R00424 96920

C0-DXA-471

CHICAGO PUBLIC LIBRARY
HAROLD WASHINGTON LIBRARY CENTER
R0042496920

FORM 125 M

EDUCATION & PHILOSOPHY

The Chicago Public Library

Received MAR 13 1985

WORLD BANK STAFF WORKING PAPERS
Number 599

Student Loans as a Means of Financing Higher Education

Lessons from International Experience

Maureen Woodhall

The World Bank
Washington, D.C., U.S.A.

Copyright © 1983
The International Bank for Reconstruction
and Development / THE WORLD BANK
1818 H Street, N.W.
Washington, D.C. 20433, U.S.A.

First printing August 1983
All rights reserved
Manufactured in the United States of America

This is a working document published informally by the World Bank. To present the results of research with the least possible delay, the typescript has not been prepared in accordance with the procedures appropriate to formal printed texts, and the World Bank accepts no responsibility for errors. The publication is supplied at a token charge to defray part of the cost of manufacture and distribution.

The views and interpretations in this document are those of the author(s) and should not be attributed to the World Bank, to its affiliated organizations, or to any individual acting on their behalf. Any maps used have been prepared solely for the convenience of the readers; the denominations used and the boundaries shown do not imply, on the part of the World Bank and its affiliates, any judgment on the legal status of any territory or any endorsement or acceptance of such boundaries.

The full range of World Bank publications is described in the *Catalog of World Bank Publications*; the continuing research program of the Bank is outlined in *World Bank Research Program: Abstracts of Current Studies*. Both booklets are updated annually; the most recent edition of each is available without charge from the Publications Distribution Unit of the Bank in Washington or from the European Office of the Bank, 66, avenue d'Iéna, 75116 Paris, France.

Maureen Woodhall is senior research officer at the Institute of Education, University of London, and a consultant to the Education Department of the World Bank.

Library of Congress Cataloging in Publication Data

Woodhall, Maureen.
  Student loans.

  (World Bank staff working papers ; no. 599)
  Bibliography: p.
  1. Student loan funds. I. Title. II. Series.
LB2340.W63 1983   378'.362   83-10611
ISBN 0-8213-0206-X

ABSTRACT

This paper examines international experience with student loans as a means of financing higher education, with particular reference to developing countries.

Experience in developed countries shows that student loan schemes can and do work. Although critics predicted that students would not be willing to borrow and that loans would discourage low-income students and women who would be frightened by the idea of a "negative dowry", there is evidence that loans are popular with students; there is no evidence that they discourage women or students from low-income families.

Evaluations of educational credit in Latin America show that student loans have been successful in increasing enrollments in many countries and have enabled poor students to enroll who could not otherwise have afforded higher education. One significant benefit is that many student loan institutions have been successful in attracting funds from such new sources as commercial banks and business enterprises. However, no student loan scheme is self-financing and because of the extent of interest subsidies and long repayment periods, student loan programs will continue to need regular injections of capital from government and other sources. As a cost-recovery mechanism, student loans do not provide immediate savings. Nevertheless, in the long run, student loans could provide a significant source of funds for higher education. The introduction of student loans will make bigger impact if it is accompanied by other changes, such as increases in tuition fees and reduction in costs.

Student loans therefore should not be regarded as a panacea, but rather as a method of finance which, when combined with tuition fees and selective scholarships can offer many advantages. The conclusion of this study is that it is feasible to introduce student loans in developing countries; they are more equitable than existing patterns of highly subsidised tuition and may contribute to greater efficiency by influencing student motivation and cost consciousness. Student loans are flexible and can be used to provide incentives for particular groups of students or to fulfill manpower objectives. Also, loans can provide a significant source of finance for higher education and vocational and technical education in the long run.

TABLE OF CONTENTS

		Page
INTRODUCTION AND SUMMARY		1

SECTION I — THE FUNCTION OF STUDENT LOANS 8

Purposes of Student Loan Programs 8
Different Types of Student Loans 9
The Extent of Subsidy of Student Loans 11

SECTION II — STUDENT LOANS IN DEVELOPED COUNTRIES 16

The Proportion of Students Receiving Financial Aid . 16
The Income Level of Aid Recipients 16
The Cost of Student Loans 17
A Revolving Fund for Student Loans 19
The Financing of Student Loan Funds 20
The Repayment of Student Loans 21
The Effect of Loans on Equality of Opportunity . . . 22
Attitudes Towards Loans 25
The Lessons for Developing Countries 26

SECTION III — EDUCATIONAL CREDIT IN LATIN AMERICA AND THE CARIBBEAN 29

The Scale of Student Loan Programs 32
Administration of Educational Credit Institutions . 37
The Financing of Student Loans 37
Repayment Terms 41
The Cost of Administering Student Loans 44
Default on Student Loans 45

SECTION IV — STUDENT LOANS IN OTHER DEVELOPING COUNTRIES 49

An Experiment in Ghana 49
Loan Schemes in Other African Countries 53
Student Loans in Asia 59
Student Loans in the Middle East 63

SECTION V — EVALUATION OF STUDENT LOANS IN DEVELOPING COUNTRIES 65

Feasibility 65
Loans as a Cost-Recovery Mechanism 69
Flexibility 70
Efficiency 71
Equity 72
Manpower 76
Administration 77

		Page
SECTION VI	THE ROLE OF INTERNATIONAL AGENCIES	78
	US Agency for International Development	78
	Inter-American Development Bank	83
	The World Bank	85
SECTION VII	THE CHOICE BETWEEN STUDENT LOANS AND OTHER METHODS OF FINANCING HIGHER EDUCATION	87
SECTION VIII	POLICY CHOICES IN DESIGNING STUDENT LOAN PROGRAMS	92
	The Trade-Off Between Costs and Selectivity	92
	The Degree of Subsidy of Student Loans	93
	Efficiency and Equity Trade-Offs	93
	The Trade-Off Between the Complexity and the Costs of Administration	94
	The Choice of Administrative Model	94
	Loan Repayment Terms	95
	The Level of Education	95
SECTION IX	FURTHER EXPERIMENTATION OR RESEARCH ON STUDENT LOANS	97
SECTION X	CONCLUSIONS	100
	The Feasibility of Student Loans in Developing Countries	100
BIBLIOGRAPHY		102
APPENDIX 1	Summary of Educational Credit Institutions in Latin America	107

INTRODUCTION AND SUMMARY

Throughout the world, students frequently borrow money to finance their education. There is nothing new in this; students in many countries have always borrowed from family or relatives to finance either the costs of tuition or their living expenses, and a few have borrowed from banks or other financial institutions, but the riskiness of lending to students who lack collateral, and who may be unable to repay the debt for many years has meant that few students are able to finance their education by borrowing, unless their families are wealthy or special loans are made available.

In the past twenty years many countries, both developed and developing, have established programs of student loans, or educational credit, to enable students to borrow, in order to invest in their own higher education. The spread of the notion of education as investment in human capital and the belief that education contributes to economic growth encouraged the idea that students should have greater access to capital markets in order to help them finance this investment. Student loans were advocated as an ideal way of ensuring that individuals of high ability but limited financial means should not be denied the educational opportunities that would lead to higher levels of personal and national income.

During the 1950's student loans were introduced on a small scale in Europe and in the United States, and also in Colombia and India. During the 1960's and 1970's student loan schemes were established, or expanded, in many developed countries, including several European countries, particularly Scandinavia and also Canada, Japan and the United States. At the same time, loan schemes were established in other Latin American countries and the Caribbean, and also in some countries in Africa and Asia. Many economists argued in favour of greater use of loans as a means of financing education, and urged international agencies and development banks to encourage the creation and development of student loan institutions. At the same time, however, other commentators were highly critical of student loans, and argued for scholarships, fellowships and grants, as a better way of providing financial aid for students, and direct subsidies to institutions, to allow them to provide free or highly subsidised tuition, as a better way for governments to ensure adequate investment in education.

In some countries, particularly the U.K., a fierce debate developed about loans versus grants. Opponents of loans argued that they would not extend opportunities, since working-class students from low-income families would be discouraged by the fear of accumulating large debts, that the costs of administering a loan program would be prohibitive, and default rates would be high. Advocates of loans, on the other hand, argued that loans were more equitable than grants, would encourage efficiency, improve motivation of students and would allow governments to assist a larger number of students with a given budget.

Similarly, in some developing countries there has been controversy about the advantages and disadvantages of student loans. Several economists have argued for greater use of student loans, as a means of reducing the financial burden of government subsidies for higher education at a time of increasing financial constraints. Others have argued that loans are more equitable than grants, since those who receive higher education will benefit by means of improved job opportunities and higher life time incomes, and should therefore contribute to the costs of their education out of their higher earnings.

During the 1970's the question of equity and the role of student loans in extending and redistributing educational opportunities was frequently emphasised. More recently, the difficulties of financing rising levels of educational expenditure have focussed more attention on the importance of student loans as a cost recovery mechanism which would allow governments to expand enrollments without imposing impossible burdens on public funds. For example, the World Bank's Education Sector Policy Paper, in 1980, pointed out that "If education systems continue to grow at the present rate and under the same structural and managerial conditions, they will require funds that - while far below those allocated to education in developed countries - will be beyond the financial capabilities of many developing countries". The two solutions that are proposed in that paper are finding additional souces of financing and reducing unit costs by improving the efficiency of the education system. A "system of fees and loans, balanced by scholarships" is suggested as one way of overcoming financial constraints in developing countries (World Bank 1980).

On the other hand, critics of loans suggest that administrative problems, particularly the problem of securing repayment, inadequacies in the banking system in many developing countries and the problem of the brain drain, make loans an inappropriate method of financing education in developing countries, and it is argued that they would be so unpopular among students that student loan schemes would not be feasible, except in rare cases.

Although this controversy has been raging, both in developed countries and developing countries, for a number of years, there has been surprising little systematic research on student loans as a means of financing education. Detailed reviews of student loan programs in Scandinavia (Woodhall 1970), in OECD countries (Woodhall 1978) and most recently in Canada, Sweden and the USA (Woodhall 1982) have shown that many lessons can be drawn from international experience with student loans in developed countries. It is more difficult to evaluate the experience of developing countries, since information about student loan programs, and critical assessments of their effectiveness in developing countries are not widely available.

OUTLINE OF THE PAPER

The purpose of this paper, therefore, is to examine international experience with student loans, with particular reference to developing countries, using published sources of information, wherever possible. The study draws on imformation collected in Sweden and the USA, and on information kindly provided by officials of the World Bank, the US Agency for International Development (AID), the Inter-American Development Bank (IDB) and the Organisation of American States (OAS) in Washington and UNESCO and the International Institute for Educatonal Planning (IIEP) in Paris. In addition, it draws on material provided for the Eighth Pan American Congress on Educational Credit, organised by the Asociacion

Panamericano de Instituciones de Credito Educativo (APICE) in Porto Allegre, Brazil, in Spetember 1979, and other data kindly provided by APICE and officials of student loan institutions in various Latin American countries, and some other developing countries. However, no field trips were attempted, and the paper therefore relies mainly on published information and evaluations of student loan programs in developing countries.

The following section provides a brief summary of the main purposes of student loan programs around the world, and describes the different types of student loans that are available, and their role in financing education. Section II looks briefly at the experience of developed countries with student loans, and draws some general conclusions about the advantages and disadvantages of loans as a means of financing higher education. The main part of the paper, however, is the description of student loan programs in Latin America, (Section III) and in other developing countries, (Section IV), and an evaluation of experience with student loans in developing countries (Section V). The role of international agencies in funding student loan institutions is examined in Section VI. Finally, the paper examines the general arguments for student loans, versus other methods of financing education, in the light of this international experience (Section VII) and there is a brief summary of the policy choices to be faced when a student loan program is established (Section VIII). The possibility of further research and experimentation in the future is discussed in Section IX. The conclusion, in Section X, evaluates the potential of student loans as a means of financing education, and argues that loans can contribute to both efficiency and equity goals in developing countries, that they are a flexible method of student support and that in the long run loans act as a cost-recovery mechanism which may contribute to a solution to the financial constraints threatening continued educational expansion in the developing world. However, student loans are not a panacea and their impact will be greater if they are combined with other financial reforms.

SUMMARY: LESSONS FROM INTERNATIONAL EXPERIENCE

Experience in developed countries, including Sweden and the USA, and also Canada, Japan and many European countries, shows that student loan schemes can and do work. In Sweden and in other Scandinavian countries a very high proportion of students receive loans, combined with grants, to finance their living expenses, while they are following free courses of higher education. In Canada, Japan and the U.S.A. students receive loans to help them finance tuition fees, as well as living expenses. In these countries student loan schemes are well established; they have been adapted, to respond to social, economic or educational changes and they have encountered problems, notably increasing costs of interest subsidies and in some cases high rates of default. But these problems can be solved, and in all the countries where loan schemes are used the government intends to continue to rely heavily on student loans in the future. Although critics predicted that students would not be willing to borrow, that loans would discourage low-income students and women, who would be frightened by the idea of a "negative dowry", there is evidence that loans are popular with students, but no evidence that they discourage women, or students from low-income families.

When most student loan schemes were introduced in developed countries, it represented an increase in financial support for students, rather than a reduction, so this experience does not provide a guide to what would happen if governments introduced loans in place of grants, or simultaneously increased tuition fees. Germany has recently increased loans in relation to grants for students, and the UK is considering substituting a combined loan-grant system for the present system which relies exclusively on grants, but few countries have reduced the level of subsidy for higher education by means of loans.

In developing countries however, where both tuition and living costs are often highly subsidized, the introduction of student loans would involve a reduction in the level of subsidy for higher education. Loans have been advocated as a way of shifting the balance between public and private financing of education which would be more equitable than the systems of free tuition and scholarships which persist in many developing countries.
However the question of the equity of loans is closely linked with the issue of tuition fees and few developing countries have yet been willing to increase tuition fees.

Student loans, or educational credit as they are often called, were first introduced in Colombia, and India and student loan programs have now spread throughout Latin America and the Caribbean and are found on a small scale in Kenya and Nigeria, India, Pakistan, Sri Lanka, Hong Kong, Eygpt and Israel. A short lived experiment in Ghana led to the introduction of student loans, combined with an increase in fees, but this scheme was abandoned after only a year, due to a change in government. However some useful conclusions can be drawn from this experience, and it does not prove that loans are infeasible in an African context. On the contrary, it demonstrates the need for careful planning and publicity if loans are introduced.

The equity implications of student loans have been emphasised in the past, but much less attention has been paid to the efficiency arguments for loans which are also important. It has been suggested that loans would improve efficiency by reducing wastage and helping to reduce the length of study, by improving student motivation and increasing cost consciousness among students. There is little evidence to support or refute these arguments, but this paper argues that loans should be evaluated in terms of their effects on efficiency as well as equity, and in terms of their capacity to generate long-term funds for education.

The review of student loan programs in Section III - V shows that there is a great variety of administrative patterns, and terms and conditions of student loans. In general, however, loans are subsidised by the government, through interest subsidies and long repayment periods. The loan schemes are designed to fulfill a number of objectives, the most important being to increase the supply of trained manpower and to widen access to higher education by removing financial barriers for poor students. In some developing countries loans are provided for tuition fees as well as living expenses, but in several countries, where tuition is free, loans are available simply for living expenses and the purchase of books. Many of the loan schemes in Latin America have received financial assistance from IDB or US AID and both agencies continue to support student loan schemes in Latin America today.

There have been certain problems with student loan programs; default rates and delayed payments have proved troublesome in some countries, but there have been improvements in collection procedures and in many countries this is no longer regarded as a very serious problem. The problem of brain drain does not seem severe. However, one problem that does deserve further study is the problem of students who do not complete their studies.

Experience also shows that it is important to distinguish between genuine defaulters and those who need to postpone repayment due to unemployment or financial problems.

Evaluations of educational credit in Latin America show that student loans have been successful in increasing enrollments in many countries, and have enabled poor students to enrol who could not otherwise have afforded higher education. One significant benefit is that many student loan institutions have been successful in attracting new sources of finance for student support, for instance from commercial banks or business enterprises. However, no student loan scheme is self-financing and because of the extent of interest subsidies and the long repayment periods, student loan programs will continue to need regular injections of capital from government or other sources, including the international agencies.

As a cost-recovery mechanism, therefore, student loans do not provide immediate savings. Nevertheless, in the long run, student loans could provide a significant source of funds for higher education.

The introduction of student loans would have greater impact if accompanied by other changes, particularly increased tuition fees, and attempts to reduce costs. A student loan program is not a substitute for cost-reduction measures designed to improve the efficiency of higher education, but should be accompanied by attempts to increase internal efficiency, and reduce waste.

Even more important, in many developing countries, is the question of tuition fees. The pattern of subsidy for higher education can be regarded as a continuum. At one extreme, would be a system of full tuition fees combined with loans. At the other extreme is a system of free tuition combined with scholarships or bursaries for living expenses. The introduction of student loans in developing countries simply involves a shift along this continuum, but to effect a major shift, most governments would have to increse the level of tuition fees substantially, as well as introducing student loans.

Many countries now recognise that to promote equality of opportunity it is necessary to provide financial support for students in other sectors of the education system. In some countries loans are now being extended to upper secondary and vocational education. However, further research needs to be done on practical questions such as the maximum burden of debt that is feasible for students, and capital ceilings for student loan institutions.

International agencies have already played an important part in providing both financial and technical assistance to student loan institutions in Latin Ameica. IBRD could now play an important role in increasing awareness of the potential of loans as a financing mechanism, in disseminating the results of research on existing loan programs and encouraging further experimentation. Experience suggests that the introduction of student loans needs very careful preparation and appropriate publicity.

Governments considering the introduction of student loans need to pay particular attention to such questions as:

1) The capital requirements of a student loan program. Experience shows that this has often been underestimated.

2) The extent of subsidy. The lower the rate of interest charged on loans, and the longer the repayment period, the greater will be the cost of subsidising loans.

3) The choice of administrative model. Some developing countries have chosen to establish state loan institutions, while others use commercial banks. The choice will depend on the conditions in the country, however the fact that commercial banks and private capital can be involved in the financing of education may be one of the main benefits of student loans in some developing countries.

4. The determination of repayment terms. It is important to establish efficient procedures for collecting repayments, for granting postponement to graduates in financial difficulties, and for dealing with defaulters. Experience shows that administrative problems have often been underestimated, but they can be solved.

5) The need to secure widespread recognition of the advantages of a loan scheme. Experience in several countries shows the importance of appropriate publicity, and the need to persuade both students and the general public of the arguments in favour of student loans.

The introduction or extension of student loans schemes in developing countries could be worthwhile in the long run, although it would not provide any quick savings for governments. The introduction of loans needs to be weighed against alternatives, such as a graduate tax, which has been suggested in some developing countries. One advantage of student loans is that they are a "multi-purpose tool" and can be a very flexible means of finance. However, it is important not to expect too much from the introduction of student loans.

The introduction of loans will not by itself solve problems of cost recovery, efficiency or equity. There are practical and administrative problems to be overcome, and no student loan scheme is likely to be fully self-financing. Nevertheless, it is recognised that to subsidise higher education by means of free tuition and scholarships or grants now imposes an increasing burden on public funds in many developing countries, and is neither efficient nor equitable. Though loans cannot solve this problem, they can contribute to a long-term solution.

Thus, student loans should not be regarded as a panacea, but as a method of finance which, when combined with tuition fees and selective scholarships has many advantages. The final conclusion of this study, therefore, is that student loans are feasible in developing countries, that they are more equitable than existing patterns of highly subsidised tuition and maintenance for a priveleged minority and may contribute to greater efficiency by influencing student motivation and cost consciousness. Student loans are flexible and can be used to provide incentives for particular groups of students or to fulfil manpower objectives. Finally, loans can provide a significant source of finance for higher education and vocational and technical education in the long run, although they will not provide quick savings.

The introduction of student loans needs to be carefully planned, accompanied by appropriate changes to fees and, if necessary by cost-reduction measures, and also by an appropriate campaign of publicity to convince both students and taxpayers of the merits of a scheme which allows students financial support today, when they need it, in return for a promise that they, in turn, will contribute directly to the financial support of the students of tomorrow.

SECTION 1.

THE FUNCTION OF STUDENT LOANS

Purposes of Student Loan Programmes.

In any country, student aid policy is designed to achieve a number of different objectives, though these are not always explicit. In the case of student loan programs, the objectives are often clearly spelled out, when the scheme is first established, but subsequent changes may give greater or less emphasis to particular aims. A further problem is that the language of student aid programs is not always clear, and different words are used to describe similar programs in different countries, while the word "loan" or "scholarship" is certainly not always used in the same way.

The main purpose of student loans, or educational credit, is to provide access for students to capital funds, to enable them to finance all, or part of, the costs of their educaton, by borrowing, while they are studying, and to repay this, at a later date. The terms "student loans" or "educational credit" refer to a system of financial aid for students which entails a repayment obligation, on the part of the student, but this obligation may take different forms. In most cases the debt must be repaid, either with or without interest, in a given period of time, and the loan therefore resembles a mortgage. In some cases the length of time of repayment may be varied, and the installments may not be of equal size. Alternatively a student may undertake to repay the debt by means of a fixed proportion of his or her future salary, an "income-contingent loan".

In some countries such aid is called a "repayable scholarship", rather than a loan, and in some countries, the repayment obligation involves a committment to work in a particular occupation (eg teaching) or in a particular region, rather than repayment in monetary terms. This type of financial assistance may be called a bonded scholarship, or a pre-salary (contrats de preembauche in France), but in the context of developing countries they have been called "service-loans" (Ciller 1975).

Student loans, or educational credit, like other forms of financial aid for students which may be called grants, scholarships, bursaries, awards, fellowships, or may consist of subsidised work opportunities, as in the College-Work-Study Program in the USA, are primarily intended to provide students with financial assistance towards the costs of tuition or maintenance. However, the fundamental difference between loans and grants is that students must repay the loan, and so contribute directly to the cost of their education, out of their subsequent earnings. Thus, a loan scheme involves less financial burden for the government, and ultimately the taxpayer, than a system of grants or scholarships.

In some cases a student loan program may simply be intended to overcome financial barriers to access, and imperfections in the capital market which make it difficult for students or their parents to obtain loans from commercial banks, because of the riskiness of the investment, the long period of the loan, or shortages of capital. An example of this kind of program is the recent introduction of PLUS loans in the USA. The acronym stands for Parents' Loans for Undergraduate Study, though PLUS loans are also available for postgraduate students. Under this program commercial banks provide loans to students who do not qualify for subsidised loans under Federal or State government loan programs. In most countries, however, student loan programs are not simply intended to overcome capital market imperfections, but to provide loans on favourable terms, usually involving a subsidy. The purpose of the subsidy may be to encourage higher education enrolment on manpower grounds, or to increase equality of opportunity, on equity grounds.

A study of Latin American education credit institutions for US AID (Herrick, et. al 1974) analyzed the stated goals of the institutions and educational credit programs in fifteen Latin American countries and concluded that the two major goals of all the programs were:-

(1) to provide the country with skilled manpower needed for social and economic development and

(2) to promote equality of opportunity for access to post-secondary education.

However, the authors observe "It became apparent that the manpower development and equality of opportunity goals at times are mutually exclusive. In other words, striving for social equity in sharing the benefits of educational opportunity might preclude the training of a greater number as rapidly as possible or vice versa" (Herrick et al 1974, p.2).

Other objectives of student loan programs include improvements in efficiency, for example by reducing wastage and drop-out among students, or increasing motivation. The study by Herrick et. al. concludes "The leadership of the education credit movement has made a positive contribution toward acceptance of the idea that the costs of higher level education should be borne by the recipients. They believe that a student receiving a loan instead of a scholarship will have a greater sense of responsibility about his education". Many programs also aim to improve student motivation by influencing their choice of subject. For example, many programs in Latin America favour science and engineering, rather than arts or humanities, on grounds of manpower needs.

DIFFERENT TYPES OF STUDENT LOANS

Most loan programs provide simple mortgage-type loans, with a fixed repayment period, usually with a "grace period" after graduation, which allows a student to find a job before embarking on repaying the loan. However, several advocates of student loans prefer an income-contingent loan, which would require a student to promise to pay a fixed proportion of future income until the loan was repaid. Such a scheme has been proposed in Canada and the USA, and Rogers has recommended it for developing countries, (Rogers, February 1971), but it has not been put into practice on a significant scale in any country, although the implications of such a scheme have been examined in the USA (Johnstone 1972).

In most countries student loans are combined with other forms of financial assistance, such as scholarships, grants, subsidised meals or boarding facilities, but in some countries, notably Japan and some Latin American countries, loans represent the main form of student aid. However, in some cases part of a student's debt may be forgiven, or written off in certain circumstances. Several loan schemes have loan forgiveness provisions for particular occupations, or categories of student. For example student loans in Honduras may be partly written off if students achieve good academic results, or work in priority areas, such as rural development projects. Such loan forgiveness clauses are not widely used, but interest in their use is growing in some Latin American countries, and some European countries (eg Germany) are also considering offering loan forgiveness provisions as an incentive to students to complete higher education more quickly.

The main difference between loan programs in different countries is the degree of subsidy involved; in some cases loans are provided interest-free, whereas other loan programs charge students a rate of interest approaching commercial rates, although in many cases interest is low or zero during the actual period of study and the "grace period" immediately after graduation.

In the USA there are various loan programs all with different rates of interest:

1) National Direct Student Loans (NDSL), originally introduced in 1958 as the National Defense Student Loan Program, intended for the poorest students.

2) Guaranteed Student Loans (GSL), established in 1965, intended for those with slightly higher incomes.

3) PLUS loans, (Parents' Loans for Undergraduate Study) introduced in 1981, also called Auxiliary Loans. These are intended for students, or their parents, who do not qualify for subsidised loans.

4) Health Education Assistance Loan (HEAL) Program, intended for medical and dental students, and other small programs for professional studies.

Very few countries take explicit account of inflation in determining the amount to be repaid, although in Sweden, when the present system of student loans was introduced in 1964, students were required to repay their loans in terms of constant purchasing power. After graduation, a students's total debt was expressed in terms of a multiple of the "base amount" which is used to determine social security payments, pensions and even student aid, and which is linked automatically with the cost-of-living index. Thus when the cost-of-living increased, the amount a student received as a loan automatically increased, but so did the amount that former students must repay. This system worked well when the rate of inflation was low, but when, in common with other developed countries, Sweden experienced a marked increase in the annual rate of inflation, students were unhappy about a system which implied an "open-ended" committment to repay. The system was therefore changed, and an annual "adjustment index" is now applied, each year, to a student's outstanding debt, and this resembles a conventional interest rate. However, if it is less than the annual rate of inflation it means that students repay their debt in nominal, but not in real terms.

In many countries student loans are provided both for tuition costs and living expenses, or maintenance costs. In the case of students attending private universities, or where public universities charge fees, this means that loans are available to help students finance their tuition fees. However, in many developing countries tuition fees have been either abolished, or are very low, so that in this case students use loans to finance living expenses or travel, purchase of books etc.

THE EXTENT OF SUBSIDY OF STUDENT LOANS

The extent to which students are subsidised varies considerably, both in terms of the amount of tuition fees and the interest they must pay on loans. In Kenya, for example, fees represent only 6 per cent of university income, in Nigeria tution fees were abolished in 1977-8, and in many African countries fees were virtually non-existent. In Latin America, even though fees are charged in some institutions, the fees cover a very small proportion of total costs, in most cases, and the majority of students in higher education are very highly subsidised, by virtue of low tuition fees, except for students in private unviersities, for example in Colombia, where fees account for 62 per cent of income and vary with respect to students' income level (Jallade 1973).

One study of the finance of education in Latin America estimated that if higher-income students were to pay the entire cost of their secondary and higher educaton, whether in the public or in the private sector, "The fiscal resources released by the adoption of such a measure would equal 14% of the present overall public expenditure on education" (IDB 1978).

In a few countries in Asia, notably Japan, and the Phillipines, tuition fees in private universities cover the full cost of tuition, but this is rare, and the general pattern is that all students, regardless of income, receive highly subsidised tuition, if they are fortunate enough to gain access to higher education.

In addition, students who receive scholarships are futher subsidised, and those who receive loans are subsidised in so far as loan repayments do not cover the full costs of servicing the loan, including interest and allowance for inflation. The interest charged on student loans varies from zero in some developing countries to 12-15 per cent in some loan programs in Canada and the U.S.A. Where students pay low rates of interest this means, in effect, that part of their loan is actually a grant. In the U.S.A. it is estimated that interest subsidies on GSLP and NDSLP in 1978 meant that between 45 and 60 per cent of each student loan was actually a "hidden grant". Dresch for example argues that "The true federal cost of a loan is equal to the amount borrowed plus the present value of all subsequent costs less the present value of all future repayment revenues. This is the cost that should be recognised at the time the loan is made.." His calculation shows that a $1,000 NDSL loan involves a grant of $596 and a loan of only $404, while the GSL program combines a grant of $456 with a loan of $544". (Dresch 1979 and 1980).

In Latin America, in 1970, interest rates charged on student loans varied from 2 per cent in Mexico to 8 per cent in Peru, and Rogers estimated that this meant that the subsidy was between 14 and 31 per cent of the value of the loan if the real interest rate in the economy is 8 per cent and between 39 and 61 per cent if the real interest rate is 16 per cent. (Rogers, February 1972). The basis for these calculations is shown in Tables 1.1 and 1.2, which show the variation in interest rates on student loans in Latin America in 1970.

During the 1970's, with the general rise in inflation and interest rates, many student loan programs increased their interest rates; for example in the USA the interest on the most subsidised loans, NDSLP, increased from 3 per cent to 5 per cent, and on GSLP loans from 6 to 9 per cent, but these still represented very substantial subsidies. Even in Canada, when the interest rate on student loans was increased to 15.3 per cent in 1981-2, it was still below market rates of interest. In most Developing countries student loans are still highly subsidised. In 1978, in most Latin American loan programs interest was between 4 and 8 per cent, although in several programs interest was 10, or 12, or even 15 per cent.

One important difference between countries which have introduced, or considered introducing, student loans, is whether or not this represented an increase or a reduction in the degree of subsidy for students. In the U.S.A., and in most Latin American countries, the introduction of student loans represented an increase in the amount of financial aid to students, but in the U.K. where the present government is considering introducing loans instead of the present system of grants, this would mean that students would have to bear a larger, not a smaller proportion of the costs of their education in the future. Similarly, when a short-lived student loan program was introduced in Ghana, it was accompanied by an increase in charges for meals and accommodation, so it meant that students were less subsidised than previously. (Further details of the Scheme in Ghana are given below).

Unfortunately, the literature on student loans does not always make clear, when there is a proposal to introduce student loans, whether this would involve increasing or reducing subsidies. In general, however the arguments put forward for greater use of student loans in developing countries imply a reduction in the level of subsidy. In many cases, the proposal to extend student loan programs in developing countries is explicity linked with proposals to increase tuition fees, thus increasing the private contribution to educational finance and reducing the burden on public funds.

CRITERIA FOR EVALUATING STUDENT LOANS

The arguments for or against student loans in developing countries must be analysed in terms of the impact of loans on:-

(i)   the level of public and private expenditure on education, and the degree of public subsidy;

(ii)   access to higher education, and the effect of loans on private demand for education;

TABLE 1.1

INTEREST RATES IN LATIN AMERICAN STUDENT LOAN INSTITUTIONS

AND OTHER NATIONAL INTEREST RATES, 1970

Country	Student Loan Interest Rate During Education	Student Loan Interest Rate Repayment	Discount Rate	National Interest Rates Commercial and Industrial Loans	Agriculture Loans	Housing Loans
Argentina	4	4	16[a]	22		16
Chile			20	39.3(real 5.1)	39.3(real 5.1)	42.1(real 7.)
Colombia	3	3	8	14-16	7-12	12-15
Costa Rica	6	6	5	8-12	9	9
Dominican Republic	5	5		12-13		9.5
Honduras	6	6	4[b]	8-12	12	9
Jamaica	6	6	6	8(Prime)		
Mexico	2	2	4.5			
Nicaragua	3	6	6	12-13	9-11	12
Panama	0	5				
Peru	8	8	9.5	9-13	7-14	10-13
Venezuela	5	5	5		6	

Source for national rates: IMF, various reports.

a. "Basic Rate"
b. "Advance" rate

Source: Rogers, February 1972, p.19

TABLE 1.2

ALTERNATIVE ESTIMATES OF INTEREST SUBSIDIES AS A PROPORTION OF TOTAL STUDENT LOANS IN HONDURAS, PANAMA and MEXICO, 1970

Assumed Real Interest Rate	Honduras	Panama	Mexico
	(interest subsidy as % of total loan)		
8	14%	31%	25%
12	28%	48%	37%
16	39%	61%	46%

Source: Rogers February 1972, p. 18

(iii) efficiency of higher education institutions, including questions of wastage and drop-out of students, as well as subject choice;

(iv) the equity of patterns of access to higher education and its financing, in other words, the question of who benefits and who pays for education.

In the next sections, student loan programs in developed and developing countries will be evaluated in the light of these criteria.

SECTION II

STUDENT LOANS IN DEVELOPED COUNTRIES

Student loans are extensively used to as a means of helping students in higher education in Canada, the U.S.A., Japan, and throughout Europe, particularly Scandinavia. In most countries loans are combined with scholarships and grants. Japan is unusual in providing virtually all financial aid in the form of loans and the UK is unusual in having no system of loans, although the British government is considering introducing a combination of grants and loans, instead of the existing system of means-tested grants. Student loans may be provided by public agencies, such as the Central Study Assistance Committee in Sweden, or by commercial banks, as in Canada, and the USA, but in most cases governments provide a guarantee for the loans, write off upaid debts in the case of death or default by a student, and also subsidise the interest a student must pay on the loan.

In most countries governments also provide indirect aid to students or their families, in the form of Subsidized meals, housing or travel, or income tax relief. Most existing systems of student aid in developed countries were introduced or expanded during the 1960's and were intended to help students finance both tuition and living costs, thus removing financial barriers to access to higher education, and promoting equality of opportunity. As well as providing aid to students, governments heavily subsidise tuition costs; fees have largely been abolished in Europe, provide less than 10 per cent of university income in Canada, and in the U.K. all home students have their fees paid in full, out of public funds, and only overseas students pay fees that are designed to cover the full costs of higher education. In Japan and the USA fees represent the main source of income for private universities, but public universities and colleges are heavily subsidized.

THE PROPORTION OF STUDENTS RECEIVING FINANCIAL AID

There are considerable differences in the proportion of students receiving aid; in Sweden and the UK, for example between 70 and 90 per cent of all students in higher education receive grants or loans, and the average award, in 1975 was 36 to 43 per cent of GDP per capita. Thus in these countries, the taxpayer not only finances free tuition for the majority of students in higher education, but covers a large part of earnings forgone as well. This is a substantial subsidy for those academically gifted enough to qualify for higher education; in countries with a less selective system of higher education, such as France, a much lower proportion of students receive scholarships or loans (15%) and the average value is less than quarter of the per capita GDP

THE INCOME LEVEL OF AID RECEIPIENTS

In most countries student aid is means-tested, although there is a tendency in many developed countries for students to be regarded as financially independent of their parents earlier than was customary some years ago. Since student loans are subsidized, most governments limit eligibility for loans to students from lower income families, but in Sweden all students are eligible for loans regardless of family income, and there is no unwillingness to borrow, even by the poorest students, as critics of loans have suggested.

In the U.S.A. subsidized loans were originally intended for lower levels of family income, and two schemes were introduced: the NDSLP, which is highly subsidized, intended for the poorest students, and the GSLP, with interest on loans 2 per cent higher than NDSLP loans, but still below market rates of interest. Until 1978 these loans were available only to students who could demonstrate financial need, but in 1978 the Middle Income Student Assistance Act (MISAA) made subsidized loans available to all.

The result was an enormous increase in the number of student borrowers and in the cost of the program to the US federal government. Between 1978 and 1981 the number of borrowers rose from one million to about 3.5 million, and the total amount lent rose from $2 billion to about $8 billion. Thus huge increase in the volume of student loans, together with rising interest rates, meant that the costs to the federal government of subsidising GSLP loans rose from $670 million in 1978 to $2.4 billion.

This led to widespread criticism of the uncontrollable costs of student loans in the USA, and the view of one commentator, that the GSLP was a "fund-eating dragon" (Morse in Rice (Ed) 1977, p.14) was widely shared by others who believed that eligibility for interest subsidies on student loans should be limited to students from low income families. This concern reflected both the desire to control public expenditure and to avoid what Gladieux describes as "the real danger that federal benefits will drift increasingly toward the relatively well-off at the expense of the poor and neediest" (Gladieux 1980). The American experience shows very clearly the dangers of governments embarking on open-ended committments, by offering unlimited access to subsidized loans.

In 1981 the Reagan administration reintroduced an income ceiling for eligibility for GSLP loans, and introduced a new form of loans, (PLUS) with 14 per cent interest, for those ineligible for interest subsidies.

THE COST OF STUDENT LOANS

The American experience after MISAA also shows clearly how easy it is for governments to underestimate the costs of introducing, or extending eligibility for subsidized student loans. No-one in the USA fully anticipated the enormous increase in student borrowing after 1978, nor the effects of rising interest rates on the cost of subsidising loans. Dresch has commented, "At its inception in the late 1960's, the privately-capitalized GSL program appeared remarkably low cost by comparison with the appropriation-dependent NDSL program. That appearance of frugality, however, was achieved primarily by deferring very substantial costs of interest subsidies and default coverage to the future. Now, more than a decade later, that future has become the present. The problem with both programs stems from the failure to appropriately recognise and quantify the costs of these programs as part of the federal budgetary process". (Dresch 1979).

In some respects this underestimation of the costs of subsidizing loans in the the USA was due to a genuine failure to forsee the increase in student borrowing and in interest rates, but Dresch argues that many of the supporters of loans in the US simply want to "use grants masquerading as loans to achieve greater public subsidisation of higher education".

There certainly seems to be a widespread failure to appreciate the full costs of subsidising student loans in developed countries, and many people have argued that the true cost of the "hidden grants", provided by interest subsidies should be calculated and publicised, so that both students, taxpayers and administrators can have a better understanding of the extent of public subsidies for higher education.

The cost of administering student loans vary between countries. Critics of student loans argue that they will be difficult and expensive to administer, but in Sweden the Central Student Assistance Committee, which is a state agency to administer student loans and other forms of assistance, calculated that in 1980-1981 the costs of administration represented only 1.8 per cent of its total expenditure on student aid.

In the USA the GSLP is administered by commercial banks and other lending institutions, but with the help of a "special allowance" paid by the federal government to compensate the lenders for the cost of administration. In 1980-1981 there were 20,000 banks or other financial institutions making Guaranteed Loans to students. The Congressional Budget Office compared this policy with the alternative government policy of providing loans directly to students, and concludes "Paying non-federal lenders to provide student loans is costly, though not necessarily more costly than providing the loans directly through a federal lender". (Congressional Budget Office, 1980).

The reason why it is necessary, in the USA, to pay commercial banks a "special allowance" to lend to students is that banks often need a financial incentive to lend to students because as the Congressional Budget Office pointed out:-

> "Despite the relatively high gross yield on student loans (about 16 per cent in 1980) many banks do not like them. Compared to other loans, collections on student loans are costly.
> (The annual cost of servicing student loans usually ranges between 1.5 per cent and 2 per cent of loan principal, compared to usual costs of between 1/4 per cent and 3/8 per cent of loan principal for servicing home mortgages, for instance). The average size of a student loan, $2,000 is much smaller than the average size of other loans, and it is often difficult to keep track of the whereabouts of students during the ten years or so of their indebtedness. Even though the federal guarantee on student loans makes them less risky than most commercial loans, it may still be costly for banks to apply and wait for reimbursement in the case of dafault". (Congressional Budget Office 1980).

In the USA there is controversy about whether it is better to use commercial banks to administer student loans and organise repayments, or alternatively to set up a government student loan bank, as in Sweden or Norway. Hartman, for example, proposed a federal government bank to provide student loans, partly to ensure sufficient liquidity, partly to increase efficiency and reduce the costs of collecting repayments: "A large share of the cost of both the NDSLP and GSLP has been for collection. Frequent billings, in small sums, to a geographically mobile population over a 10-year period are a collector's nightmare". Hartman's suggestion was for a national bank which could use the Internal Revenue Service as collector; "only the IRS could collect this type of loan with minimal costs". (Hartman, 1971).

However, no country yet uses the income tax or inland revenue system to collect student loan repayments, and it is recognised that the costs of organising repayment, chasing defaulters, and administering the loan will be higher in the case of student loans than many other types of loan, and the costs of administration and servicing loans must be calculated accurately and included in any estimate of the costs of student loans.

A REVOLVING FUND FOR STUDENT LOANS

The cost of servicing student loans is crucial to the question of whether student loan systems can ever become fully self-financing. Many governments recognise that they will not, because of the policy of charging students less than commercial interest rates, and because of government guarantees to write off debts if students are unable to repay due to death, illness or financial hardship, or in cases of default.

Critics of loans frequently mention the problem of defaults, and the cost, to the government of providing loan guarantees, but in Canada, the Federal-Provincial Task Force on Student Assistance, which reported in 1980 concluded: "The direct costs to government of providing non-repayable aid in the form of interest subsidies is in the order of three times the amount spent on paying claims for loans to lenders under the guarantee. The problem is not in providing both sorts of assistance, but rather in having both elements entangled in a way that makes it difficult to determine how much non-repayable aid is being provided in particular cases and what is the true cost of borrowing. For example, if repayable and non-repayable elements could be kept separate, students would know clearly the interest charges that were being paid on their behalf. Government policies and programs could be more easily examined and evaluated if it were clearer how much was being spent on non-repayable aid in the form of interest subsidies and how much on loan guarantees," (Council of Minister of Education, Canada, 1980).

It is difficult to calculate accurately the proportion of loan capital that will, eventually, be recovered from loan repayments, since many schemes have expanded so rapidly in the 1970's that current levels of loan repayments cover only a small proportion of total lending. In Sweden, for example, where students have until their fiftieth birthday to repay their loans, repayments in 1981 amounted to only about one quarter of the total value of new student loans in 1980-1981. This is because most students have twenty years in which to repay their loans, they are automatically allowed to postpone repayment if their income falls below a minimum limit, so that it will take the government a very long time to recover the debt, and the annual "adjustment index" is less than market interest rates or inflation. Moreover, the volume of student loans has inreased rapidly, so that it is inevitable that current repayments cover only a small proportion of total lending.

On the other hand, it is clear that in the long run a system of loans imposes much less burden on public funds than a system of grants. Either this can be seen as a saving of public funds, or as freeing government spending for alternative uses. In Sweden the amount of loan repayments in 1981 were approximately equal to the amount spent on giving grants to adults taking short courses of further education or training.

In Denmark, calculations of the amount of loans that would eventually be recovered from loan repayments range from 22 to 70 per cent, according to alternative assumptions about the degree of interest subsidies, the rate of inflation and the length of repayment period. (Woodhall 1970). This shows clearly that the extent to which a loan system will become self-financing is a policy decision, and depends on the level of interest subsidy provided by the government.

THE FINANCING OF STUDENT LOAN FUNDS.

If student loan systems are not self-financing, even in the long run, there will always be a need for recapitalisation of the loan fund, and in any case, the long duration of the repayment period means that there will inevitably be a need for new funds before the loan repayments have built up.

In Sweden, where loans are provided by a government agency the government provides the capital as well as guaranteeing the loans and paying the costs of administraton. The Central Study Assistance Committee also provides grants, for secondary school pupils and for adults taking short courses of further education or training, or studying part-time. These grants to adults are financed by means of a pay-roll tax, but all other expenditure on grants and loans is financed out of general government revenue.

In the U.S.A. where 3.5 million students borrowed GSLP loans in 1981, the need for funding the huge volume of student loans has sometmes raised difficulties. The federal government provides the capital for NDSLP loans, but in the case of GSLP loans commercial banks provide the capital, with a guarantee from federal government or state government guarantee agencies, and a "special allowance" paid by the Federal government. This was first introduced in 1969 to encourage more banks to lend to students as rising interest rates were causing a shortage of lenders. As interest rates continued to rise in the early 1970's there was still a shortage of banks willing to lend to students, and the government created a secondary market in student loans, the Student Loan Marketing Association (Sallie Mae) which increased funding for student loans by making it possible for banks to sell or borrow against their outstanding student loans.

Since Sallie Mae was established in 1972 it has provided $6.6 billion for lenders, which has considerably increased the liquidity of the

GSLP. In 1981, it provided $2.5 billion to 1,200 banks or other lenders, either through purchase of student loans from banks, or lending, and the loans bought by Sallie Mae represent 28 per cent of all outstanding GSLP loans. Sallie Mae is a privately owned, profit-making institution; the stockholders are all educational or financial institutions. Recently Sallie Mae has widened its activities to include innovations such as "interest-rate swaps" with other financial institutions, and has introduced a Consolidation Program under which students with more than one loan, or with very large loans can negotiate repayment terms with Sallie Mae.

Such activities are clearly dependent upon sophisticated banking systems and techniques which would not be appropriate for developing countries, but this example of the creation of a new, secondary market for student loans in the USA shows that the banking system may be able to contribute significantly to the recapitalisation of student loan programs. The following section will provide examples of how commercial banks in Latin America are contributing to the financing of student loans.

The lesson for both developed and developing countries is that it is not necessary for student loan systems to rely exclusively on public funds for capitalisation.

THE PAYMENT OF STUDENT LOANS.

The length of repayment, the interest rate and other repayment terms vary considerably in different loan programs. The longest period for repayment is in Sweden, where students have a "grace period" of two years, after completing a course, and then have until their 50th birthday in which to repay; thus many students have 20 years in which to repay their loans. In addition, there are a number of automatic safeguards designed to prevent hardship for those repaying loans.

Anyone whose income falls below a minimum level (S.kr 58,450 or $12,000 in 1981) can automatically defer repayment for a year. Any outstanding debt is written off at the age of 65, or in the case of death or permanent disability, and in certain special cases part of a student's debt may be written off. For example, someone attending higher education who has previously received a loan towards the costs of upper secondary education, and has worked (or looked after a child) for at least four years may be entitled to cancellation of part of the debt for the period of upper secondary education.

This built-in "insurance element" in the Swedish system is extremely important, and helps to reduce default rates, since anyone with a very low income can automatically postpone repayment. About 10 per cent of all borrowers do postpone payment, and probably only about 1 per cent actually default on their loans.

If a student borrowed the maximum loan available for four years, the total debt (in terms of 1981 prices) would be S.kr. 84,836 (about $17,500) Table 2.1. shows how such a debt would be repaid over twenty years.

The method of calculating repayment in Sweden means that the annual payments rise gradually over the repayment period. The annual payment is calculated by dividing the total debt by the repayment period, and at the end of each year an "adjustment index" (currently 4.2 per cent) is applied, which increases the remaining debt. Thus, a debt of S.kr.84,836 to be repaid in 20 years means that in the first year the payment is S.kr. 4,242. After the "adjustment", the remaining debt of S.kr. 83,173 is divided by 19 to give the second year payment of S.kr. 4,378. (See Table 2.1.)

In Japan, the interest rate rises during the repayment period, which also means that payments increase as the graduate gets older, but in some countries the annual payments are fixed throughout the repayment period, and in the U.S.A. graduates with a particularly large loans may choose between alternative repayment methods and periods, between 10 and 20 years (See Table 2.2).

The lesson from these experiences is that it is possible to devise flexible repayment schedules, to allow for variations in size of debt, or income level, but if the loans are subsidized this will increase the cost of the loan scheme to the government.

The problem of default, which is widely discussed by critics of student loans has not proved serious in Sweden, but among some students it has proved a serious problem in the USA. The problem has been well-publicised, which has helped to reduce confidence in student loans as a financing mechanism, but in fact since 1977 default rates have been reduced by a series of vigorous government campaigns to improve collection procedures, and far more attention is now being paid to the problem of default, for example identifying particular institutions where default rates are high. In 1978, for example, the outstanding amount on NDSLP loans in default, as a percentage of total outstanding debt, varied from 14 per cent in private universities to nearly 35 per cent in public, two year colleges. A study of causes of default showed that "students attending 100 or 80 institutions account for more than half of all defaults... concentrating efforts at these institutions.... could lead to significant reductions in the default rate". (Hauptman in Rice,(Ed) 1977).

Although default rates do pose a problem in the USA this problem is by no means insoluble. If, instead of emphasising problems of defaulters, American student loan administrators stressed that "currently approximately 93 per cent of all GSLP leans that have entered repayment status are either in repayment or have been fully paid off" (Congressional Budget Office, 1980), it might increase confidence in loans as a financing mechanism. The Swedish experience also shows that if low- income earners are automatically allowed to postpone repayment, the number of actual defaulters is very low.

THE EFFECT OF LOANS ON EQUALITY OF OPPORTUNITY.

Research on the effects of student aid on equality of opportunity in higher education in developed countries suggests that neither grants or loans have had as much effect on widening opportunities, as was hoped when the schemes were introduced. American research concludes either that "loan programs have made only a modest contribution towards the goal of equal enrolment rates" (Hartman 1971) or more recently "the expansion of federal

TABLE 2.1

Example of Repayment of Student Loans in Sweden, 1981

S.Kr.

Year	Total debt 1st January	Annual Payment	Total debt after payment	'Adjustment Index Increase 3.2%	Total 31st December
1.	84,836	4,242	80,594	2,579	83,173
2.	83,173	4,378	78,795	2,521	81,316
3.	81,316	4,518	76,798	2,458	79,256
4.	79,256	4,663	74,593	2,387	76,980
5.	76,980	4,812	72,168	2,309	74,477
6.	74,477	4,966	69,511	2,224	71,735
7.	71,735	5,125	66,610	2,132	68,742
8.	68,742	5,289	63,453	2,030	65,483
9.	65,483	5,458	60,025	1,921	61,946
10.	61,946	5,633	56,313	1,802	58,115
11.	58,115	5,813	52,302	1,674	53,976
12.	53,976	5,999	47,977	1,535	49,512
13.	49,512	6,191	43,321	1,386	44,707
14.	44,707	6,389	38,318	1,226	39,544
15.	39,544	6,593	32,951	1,054	34,005
16.	34,005	6,804	27,201	870	28,071
17.	28,071	7,022	21,049	674	21,723
18.	21,723	7,247	14,476	463	14,939
19.	14,939	7,479	7,460	239	7,699
20.	7,699	7,699	0	0	0
		116,320		31,484	

Source: Central Study Assistance Committee (Sweden)

TABLE 2.2

ALTERNATIVE REPAYMENT SCHEDULES FOR GSLP LOANS, USA, 1982

Total Loan Amount		Maximum Term (in months)	First Payment	Midpoint Payment	Final Payment
$5,000	Option 1 (Level)	120	$58	$58	$58
	Option 2 (Graduated)	120	39	59	90
	Option 3 (Accelerated)	96	39	80	116
$10,000	Option 1 (Level)	156	$98	$98	$98
	Option 2 (Graduated)	156	70	105	156
	Option 3 (Accelerated)	127	70	109	214
$15,000	Option 1 (Level)	192	$130	$130	$130
	Option 2 (Graduated)	192	98	130	189
	Option 3 (Accelerated)	161	98	152	236
$20,000	Option 1 (Level)	240	$155	$155	$155
	Option 2 (Graduated)	240	125	160	216
	Option 3 (Accelerated)	207	125	179	256

Source: Sallie Mae (USA)

financial aid programs and their targeting towards youth from lower income and lower status families did not alter to any appreciable degree the composition of the post-secondary education students or college enrollment expectations... over the 1970's.... We are forced to conclude that student financial aid simply operated as a transfer program - that by substituting public for private funds it reduced the financial burden of college for parents and students without inducing additional enrolments, or even changing the mix of present enrollments". (Lee Hansen 1982).

Opponents of loans argue that grants are more effective in encouraging participation by low-income students but in Canada the Task-Force on Student Aid observed that "There is growing, but not conclusive, evidence that the form which the aid takes may not be especially important in increasing participation of students from lower income families.....loans are likely to be almost as effective in this respect as grants". (Council of Ministers, Canada, 1980).

One reason why neither loans nor grants have had as much impact on equality of opportunity as was hoped is that the barriers to access are frequently at the secondary level, rather than at the point of entry to higher education. This is why in Sweden, for example, the student aid system is giving greater priority to grants for secondary school pupils, and providing loans for students in higher education.

It is even more true in developing countries that financial barriers to access are often more important at the secondary level than in higher education itself, which is why various proposals have been made for greater use of loans in higher education, since loans can free resources for primary and secondary education.

ATTITUDES TOWARDS LOANS.

Critics of loans frequently argue that they will be unpopular with students, who will be unwilling to go into debt to pay for education. Obviously, the attitude of students depends partly on whether loans represent an extension or a reduction of financial aid and subsidy. However, in developed countries there is no evidence of reluctance to borrow. In the USA, when the first loan scheme was introduced, "the idea that students would'nt borrow was accepted as gospel. One reason was undoubtedly that few going to college had ever been asked or expected to borrow. No-one had promoted or publicized loans as a device for financing education". Yet the response was the "astonishing eagerness of students to borrow", which has continued to this day. (Morse in Rice (Ed) 1977, p.6 and 11).

Surveys in Canada and Sweden, where loan schemes are well established, show that they are popular with students, and in Canada a survey of students showed that 84 per cent preferred a combination of loans and grants, or loans alone, rather than a system based entirely on grants. (Council of Ministers, Canada 1980).

The president of the Swedish National Union of Students in 1980 said "The great majority of Swedish students want to maintain the loan system, we think it works very well... we see education as an investment in our own future, and its only natural that we should pay for that investment ourselves" (Woodhall 1982)

THE LESSONS FOR DEVELOPING COUNTRIES

The first, obvious lesson from the experience of developed countries is that loan schemes can be made to work successfully. They are not without problems, for example inflation and rising interest rates have driven up the costs of loans, both for governments and for borrowers, and default rates are sometimes uncomfortably high. Yet experience shows that these problems can be solved. Perhaps the greatest danger is underestimation of the costs of loans particularly if eligibility for loan subsidies is not strictly limited.

One advantage of loans is that they offer a more flexible system of student aid than grants alone, since the level of subsidy, the period and terms of repayment can all be adjusted, in the light of efficiency or equity objectives. Recent attempts to make repayment terms more flexible, for example by providing incentives for completing a course in below-average time, in Germany, by providing safeguards for low-earners in Sweden, or by offering a choice of repayment terms to students with large debts in the USA all emphasise the potential flexibility of loans as a financing mechanism.

Experience in developed countries shows, all too clearly, the dangers of open-ended committments, whether in providing mandatory grants, as in the UK, or subsidised loans as in the USA. There is a growing realisation that financial constraints make it necessary for governments to be more selective in student aid policy. This, too, is a valuable lesson for developing countries. Student Loans allow governments to subsidise more students with a given budget, because today's students will eventually contribute to the cost of educating the students of tomorrow.

However, there is a clear lesson about the potential savings of introducing student loans. Experience with loan schemes show that there are no quick savings to be gained from introducing loans. This would be true even if loans were accompanied by the introduction of fees, since it takes many years for loan repayments to build up sufficiently to contribute substantial revenue. However, long-run savings should not be despised because there are no short-run benefits. Calculations in Canada, reproduced in Table 2.3 show clearly that there will be long-run savings if loans are used, rather than grants. Loan repayments already contribute a quarter of Sweden's student aid budget, which reduces the burden on public funds.

American experience also shows that in a developed country the commercial banking system can contribute significantly to the funding of student loans, thus reducing the burden on public funds, although the successful participation of commercial banks in the U.S. does entail substantial public subsidies, which have been underestimated in the past. Whether or not commercial banks can play a significant part in developing countries will be examined in the following sections of the paper.

Many observers believe that loans are more equitable as a means of financing higher education in developed countries, than a system of grants which transfer purchasing power from taxpayers to those who, in the

TABLE 2.3

ESTIMATED COSTS OF ALTERNATIVE COMBINATIONS OF GRANTS AND LOANS, CANADA, 1981-82

Program mix	Estimated cost 1981-82 $ Canadian	Costs as a per cent of present mix
1979-80 mix of loans and grants	400,000,000	100
100% loans	215,000,000	54
75% loans/25% grants	335,000,000	84
50% loan/50% grants	455,000,000	114
25% loan/75% grants	575,000,000	144
100% grant	690,000,000	173
First $1000 of need is a loan and remainder is 75% loan, 25% grant	330,000,000	83
First $1000 of need is a loan and remainder is 50% loan, 50% grant	445,000,000	111
First $1000 of need is a loan and remainder 25% loan, 75% grant	535,000,000	134
First $1000 is grant and remainder is 75% grant, 25% loan	575,000,000	144
First $1000 is a grant and remainder is 50% grant, 50% loan	465,000,000	116
First $1000 is a grant and remainder is 25% grant, 75% loan	375,000,000	94

Source: Council of Minister, Canada 1980, p.136

future, will have higher than average earnings as a result of their education.

Students in universities are likely, in any case, to come from upper income families. Blaug for example, argues that in the UK "it is fair to say that almost half of the grants system simply gives to those who already have. There is nothing wrong with this if we really believe in supporting an educational elite. But to defend grants in higher education on grounds of social equality is a monstrous perversion of the truth. (Blaug, 1972, p.296). Experience in developed countries suggests that if governments really want to promote equality of opportunity in high education they must break down financial barriers at the secondary level. At the university level, loans appear to be as effective as grants, and are more equitable in terms of income redistribution.

The final judgement on student loans in developed countries can perhaps be summed up by the conclusion of the U.S. House of Representatives Committee on Education and Labor : "The student loan program is not an unmixed blessing, nor an entirely unmitigated evil... In today's fiscal and educational policy circumstances, loans are needed. Our task is to so improve the structure of the existing program as to maximise its service to students and minimise the possibility of abuse" (Rice 1977).

SECTION III

EDUCATIONAL CREDIT IN LATIN AMERICA AND THE CARIBBEAN

The idea of educational credit in Latin America was first developed in Colombia, by Dr. Gabriel Betancur Mejia, who wrote a thesis in 1943, on a "Project for the Creation of a Colombian Institute for Advanced Training Abroad", as a result of his own experience in borrowing in order to finance his postgraduate education in the USA. Acting on this idea, Betancur established, in 1950, an institution in Colombia which still bears that name, Instituto Colombiano de Credito Educativo y Estudios Tecnicos en el Exterior (ICETEX), although since the mid 1960's it has provided loans for study in Colombia as well as abroad. Table 3.1. shows how ICTEX has developed since its first loans were awarded in 1953.

One survey of student loan institutions in developing countries concludes that "the idea of national credit institutions is indigenous to Latin America - an original answer to a genuine national problem" (Dominguez 1973, p.41). Whether or not this is true, student loan institutions - called educational credit institutions throughout Latin America - have multiplied more rapidly in Latin America and the Caribbean during the 1960's and 1970's than in any other region. By 1978 there were national loan institutions in at least eighteen countries in Latin America and the Caribbean, as well as a small Pan-American fund, administered by the Oganisation of American States (OAS) and a Student Loan Scheme, established by the Caribbean Development Bank for eleven small Caribbean countries.

Student loan programs now exist in the following countries:-

1. Argentina.
2. Bolivia.
3. Barbados.
4. Brazil.
5. Colombia.
6. Costa Rica.
7. Chile.
8. Ecuador.
9. El Salvador.
10. Honduras.
11. Jamaica.
12. Mexico.
13. Nicaragua.
14. Panama.
15. Peru.
16. Dominican Republic.
17. Trinidad and Tobago.
18. Venezuela.

Many countries have established a national student loan institution, to provide and administer loans, and many of these have been partially funded by international agencies, particularly IDB, and AID. Another important form of international co-operation was the establishment, in 1969, of the Pan-American Association of Educational Credit Associatons (APICE) whose aims are "to foster the development of

TABLE 3.1

GROWTH OF ICETEX, 1953-1981

No OF STUDENT LOANS AWARDED

	For Study Abroad	For Study in Colombia
1953	74	-
1958	217	177
1963	277	907
1968	751	3,780
1973	280	14,145
1978	741	21,639
1981	619	26,371

Source: ICETEX, Informe de Labores 1981.

national and international systems for the financing of higher education using the student loan model, with the participation of the public and private sectors of the economy, in order to provide equality of opportunities to students, so that they can contribute to the cultural, economic and social transformation of their respective countries". (APICE 1981). In addition to providing technical assistance to student loan institutions APICE holds a Pan-American Congress on Educational Credit every two years, technical seminars to help with the training of institution staff and organises the exchange of information on educational credit.

There are also a number of private loan schemes, for example in Brazil there are loan programs run by trade unions and commercial banks, as well as a national fund, and several Mexican universities and the Catholic University in Chile run their own loan schemes.

Some of these loan institutions produce regular reports and APICE publishes an Information Bulletin, Journal and a Bibliography, all in Spanish. There have been a number of surveys of student loan schemes in Latn America, for example, Rogers (March 1971 and February 1972), Dominguez (1973) Herrick et al (1974), IDB (1976), Arbelaez (in Brodersohn and Sanjurjo 1978) and UNESCO (1979). Many of these are in English, but some information is available only in Spanish or Portugese.

This section draws on all these sources, in order to give a general picture of the experience with student loans in Latin America and the Caribbean, and an evaluation of this experience is provided in Section V. More detailed information on student loans in particular countries is given in many of the publications listed in the bibliography. Appendix 1 gives a summary table, which outlines the main characteristics of the student loan institutions in sixteen Latin Ameican countries in 1978.

All the loan programs share similar aims, although there are differences in emphasis in different countries. The main objectives of all the loan schemes are:-

(1) To provide continuing source of finance for higher education.

(2) To contribute to national development by encouraging investment in education to fulfil manpower needs.

(3) To promote equality of opportunity, by making it possible for poor students to finance their own education and pay for it, later, out of their enhanced earnings.

A recent summary of the idea of educational credit in Latin America for example, justified it on the following grounds:-

(1) "Educated persons are the foundation for the social and economic development of a country".

(2) "Due to the inability of many governments and of students themselves to finance their education, particularly at the university level, because of increasing enrollment as well

as the rising costs of education, it is believed that the establishment of the loan program would not only make funds more readily accessible to needy students, but also more socially equitable.

(3) "Educational credit can be converted into a long-range mechanism for securing the financing for and regulation of certain levels and types of technical and professional training".

(Ocampo 1982)

Educational credit is provided both for tuition costs (including fees where they are charged) and maintenance costs. Loans are given both for study within a country or study abroad, in most cases. In some countries, education credit institutions are solely concerned with student loans, while in other cases their functions include administration of other financial aid programs, such as scholarships and fellowships, in several cases, and free school-meals in Brazil. Some also carry out research. Certain programs are more concerned with manpower needs, while others emphasise the equity argument, but all are concerned to meet the need for a long-run financing mechanism which does not impose too heavy a burden on government funds.

THE SCALE OF STUDENT LOAN PROGRAMS

The size of the programs varies considerably from a few hundred loans a year to many thousand. Table 3.2 shows the number of loans awarded between 1976 and 1978 by the main educational credit institutions in Brazil, Colombia, Ecuador, Panama and Venezuela, together with the number of students in 1978. This shows that both in terms of the number of loans and the proportion of students assisted, the programs in Brazil and Colombia are far bigger than the other three. Table 3.3 shows the number of loans awarded in 1981 by the Student Loan Scheme of the Caribbean Development Bank.

Jallade estimated that between 1969 and 1974, about ten per cent of all students in Colombia were able to finance their studies by means of loans, while Kausel, (in IDB 1978) calculates that in 1975 about 8 per cent of all students in Colombia received ICETEX loans. This is higher than the proportion aided by Educredito in Venezuela, or Honduras where only about 2 per cent receive loans, according to Walter Ross (in IDB 1978); on the other hand he states that 26 per cent of the university population in Jamaica obtain loans.

To give an idea of the entire scale of educational credit in Latin America, and its very rapid increase in recent years, Table 3.4 shows the total number of outstanding loans in 16 Latin American countries in 1978, and Table 3.5 shows the total amount of outstanding debt (in US$) and the proportion of debt that was in the process of being repaid, compared with the proportion of loans that had not yet reached repayment status in 1978.

This shows how relatively recent much of the educational credit in Latin America is. In Honduras more than half and in Colombia and Bolivia amost a half of all outstanding debts are in the process of being

TABLE 3.2

NUMBER OF STUDENT LOANS AWARDED IN BRAZIL, COLOMBIA, ECUADOR, PANAMA & VENEZUELA 1976-8

Country	Total No. of Students in Higher Education, 1978	No. of Students Receiving Loans 1976-8
Brazil (FNDE)	1,251,116	388,415
Colombia (ICETEX)	211,302	56,422
Ecuador (IECE)	235,274	14,271
Panama (IFARHU)	34,302	4,502
Venezuela (Educredito)	282,074	2,202

Source: (1) UNESCO Statistical Yearbook 1981
(2) UNESCO 1979

TABLE 3.3

STUDENT LOAN SCHEME OF THE CARIBBEAN DEVELOPMENT BANK, 1981

COUNTRY	Student Loans Awarded	
	No.	$
Antigua	79	318
Belize	69	337
British Virgin Islands	39	107
Cayman Islands	22	129
Dominica	123	323
Grenada	70	174
Montserrat	15	32
St. Kitts/Nevis	24	-
St. Lucia	256	550
St. Vincent	98	406
Turks and Caicos	-	-
Total	795	2,376

Source: Caribbean Development Bank

TABLE 3.4

TOTAL NUMBER OF OUTSTANDING STUDENT LOANS, LATIN AMERICA 1978

Country	Total Loans awarded excluding loans already repaid
Argentina (INCE)	1,400
Bolivia (CIDEP)	476
Brazil: (APLUB)	3,084
(Caixa Economica Federal)	354,588
Colombia (ICETEX)	53,865
Costa Rica (CONAPE)	1,286
Chile (Catholic University)	1,982
Ecuador (IECE)	15,803
El Salvador (Educredito)	2,350
Honduras (Educredito)	1,740
Jamaica (Students' Loan Bureau)	6,875
Nicaragua (Educredito)	630
Panama (IFARHU)	5,800
Peru (INABEC)	274
Dominican Republic (FCE)	10,097
Venezuela (Educredito)	2,866
(SACUEDO)	2,770

Source: APICE Viii Congresso Pan Americano de Credito Educativo, 1979.

TABLE 3.5

PROPORTION OF OUSTANDING STUDENT LOANS DUE FOR REPAYMENT

LATIN AMERICA 1978

Country	% of Loans Due for Repayment.	Not yet Due
Argentina (INCE)	14.2	85.7
Bolivia (CIDEP)	46.4	53.6
Brazil (APLUB)	37.7	62.2
(Caixa Economica Federal)	3.0	97.0
Colombia (ICETEX)	44.3	55.6
Costa Rica (CONAPE)	3.4	96.5
Chile (Catholic University)	46.4	53.7
Ecuador (IECE)	24.4	75.5
El Salvador (Educredito)	43.0	57.0
Honduras (Educredito)	52.8	47.1
Jamaica (Students' Loan Bureau)	33.3	66.6
Mexico (Bank of Mexico)	71.5	28.4
Nicaragua (Educredito)	47.1	52.9
Panama (IFARHU)	36.7	63.2
Peru (INABEC)	52.5	47.4
Dominican Republic (FCE)	82.7	17.3
Venezuela (Educredito)	36.8	63.1
(SACUEDO)	7.2	92.7

Source: APICE (As Table 3.4)

repaid, whereas in Brazil and Costa Rica it is only 3 per cent. This makes it very diffiuclt to evaluate the more recent schemes in terms of repayment and default rates, since such a large proportion of their loans have not yet reached repayment stage.

ADMINISTRATION OF EDUCATIONAL CREDIT INSTITUTIONS

There is no general pattern of administration. Some of the student loan institutions, such as ICETEX in Colombia, the Instituto Nacional de Credit Educativo (INCE) in Argentina, the Fondo Nacional de Desarrollo de la Educacion (FNDE) in Brazil are public institutions, established as autonomous agencies. Educredito in Honduras was established as a private, non-profit institution in 1968, but became an autonomous public institute in 1976, whereas Educredito in Venezuela is still a private institution. In some countries, however, student loan programs are administered within national banks, for example in Mexico, a student loan fund is administered by the Bank of Mexico, on the basis of an agreement between the Bank and the Federal government of Mexico, and similarly in Jamaica, the Student Loan Fund is administered by the Bank of Jamaica.

There are also numerous private loan institutions. In Brazil there is a private, non-profit institution, set up by a trade union, the Associacao dos Profissionais Liberais Universitarios de Brasil (APLUB), which administers the APLUB Foundation for Educational Credit, and there is a semi-independent agency, within the Ministry of Labor and Social Security which provides loans and scholarships to the dependents of trade union members (PEBE)

There are also private loan funds administered by individual universities, for example the Catholic University in Chile and Sociedad Administradora de Credito Educativo para la Universidad de Oriente (SACUEDO) in Venezuela. In Costa Rica there is a fund, Departmento de Formento Nacional de Prestamos para Educacion (FONAPE) which is administered by a commercial bank.

Thus there are considerable variations in the formal structure of loan institutions in Latin America, and this is matched by considerable differences in the way they are funded.

THE FINANCING OF STUDENT LOANS

In most of the national educational credit programs government is a major source of funds, but in some cases the finance comes from general government revenue, in others there are ear-marked taxes for educational credit. Many of the institutions have received loans from IBD or AID, but in such cases the national government is required to contribute to the financing through matching funds, or in some other way. Central or commercial banks are a major source of funds in Costa Rica, Mexico, Colombia and Jamaica. There are also a number of non-traditional sources of funds, including national lotteries. Private donations are significant in some counries, and these are often encouraged by governments through fiscal incentives.

Finally, loan repayments provide some of the finance though the proportion varies, and is very small in some of the newer institutions. Kausel (in IDB 1978) suggests that even in the case of ICETEX, the oldest institution in Latin America, repayments of past loans did not amount to more than 6 per cent of total income in 1978 whereas Dr. Gabriel Betancur Mejia, the founder of ICETEX states that the proportion is about 20 per cent (Betancur, shown in Table 3.6.)

Table 3.6 shows that the major source of finance for ICETEX is the government, followed by loans from commercial banks, which, as a result of a resolution of the Central Bank are authorised to make rediscountable loans to ICETEX at only 2 per cent interest (Jallade 1974). In addition, ICETEX administers funds for private and public enterprises, and uses this money to finance loans for professional and technical training.

In Argentina, INCE receives half its funds from the government and half from commercial banks. In Brazil national lotteries contribute to the financing of two loan funds, administered by FNDE and by the Federal Savings Bank (Caixa Economica Federal), and the state-owned oil company, Petroleo Brasileiro, also contributes to their financing. Oil revenues are also an important source of finance in Ecuador, where a payroll tax also contributes to Instituto Ecuatoriano de Credito Educativo (IEC), while in El Salvador there is a loan fund financed entirely by the Central Bank.

Rogers, surveying Latin American student loan programs in 1972 pointed out "For several of the student loan programs the financial picture is dominated by loans from international aid agencies" (Rogers, February 1972, p.20). Barbados, Colombia, Costa Rica, Dominican Republic, Honduras, Jamaica, Panama, Trinidad and Tobago have all received loans from AID or IDB and their role will be examined in Section VI.

One lesson from this great variety of financing patterns for educational credit institutions in Latin America is that many of them have been able to exploit non-traditional sources of revenue, including private contributions, such as donations, loans from commercial banks, national lotteries and other public and private sources. Many countries use payroll taxes to finance technical and vocational educaton, for example Argentina (CONET), Brazil (SENAI), Colombia (SENA), Ecuador (SECAP), Guatemala (INTECAP), Honduras (INFOP), Paraguay (SNPP), Peru (SENATI), and Venezuela (INCE). (Brodersohn in IDB, 1978). Some of these taxes are used to finance loans for technical education, but the bulk of this money goes to direct grants for institutions carrying out vocational training. The study by Herrick et al (1974) lists the following sources of funds for educational credit insitutions:

Source	Used by
Regular contributions from government budget.	Colombia, Agentina, Dominican Republic
Loans from government	Honduras
External loans	Brazil, Colombia, Dominican Republic, Honduras, Nicaragua,

TABLE 3.6

SOURCES OF FINANCE FOR ICETEX, 1979

Source	Income $(000)	(%)
Government Budget.	236,340	32.6
Administration of Enterprise Funds.	132,752	18.3
Bank Loans	140,000	19.3
Central Bank	35,156	4.9
IDB	34,000	4.7
Loan Repayments	146,832	20.2
TOTAL	725,080	100.0

Source: Betancur Meija, G.

Source	Used by
External loans	Panama and Peru
Special government grants.	Dominican Republic.
Discounted bank loans	Colombia, Argentina
Fees for administration of particular programs and other services.	Colombia, Dominican Republic.
Income from short-term Investments.	Colombia, Dominican Republic, Honduras.
Interest and repayments on student loans.	All (interest is at subsidized rates)
Private donations.	Many
Allocation of oil revenues	Ecuador
Compulsory payroll deduction matched by government contribution	Panama

(Herrick et.at. 1974, p.23)

However, none of the institutions is yet able to rely on past loan repayments for a substantial part of its funds. Herrick et.al. (1974) concludes, on the basis of the early experience of many institutions:

"The creation of a revolving student loan fund - that is, one that can sustain a given annual level of lending to students from its own resources (consisting of interest and principle payments on prior loans and other regular sources of income to cover administrative costs) requires between 10 and 20 years. Education credit institutions and their external supporters in the past have projected achievement of a revolving fund capability within five to ten years, but experience shows that longer periods may be required.

The experience of the oldest, largest and most successful programe, ICETEX in Colombia, shows continually increasing government subsidies with no predictable end in sight. Although the original program of foreign study loans has been reduced, ICETEX has been given new responsibilities for higher levels of student credit, secondary school scholarships and execution of international donors' programs, and has required larger infusions of government funds. To the extent that these requirements represent a shift from government grant programs to expanding revolving loan programs or represent policies to foster greater social equity in educatonal benefits, this lack of self-sufficiency should be acceptable. A conclusion from this example may well be, however, that the more successful an Educational Credit Institution is, the less likely it is to become self-sufficient for an indeterminate time".

(Herrick et al. 1974 pp. 24-5)

Similar conclusions are drawn by many of the other surveys of Latin American experience: "Practical experience in Latin America indicates that so far the objective of a self-financing student loan fund has not been attained because the lending institutions are continually in need of infusions of government capital." (Brodersohn in IDB, 1978, p. 163) "There is not much likelihood of student loan funds becoming entirely self-sufficient, as the period of full loan recovery set in, unless additional financing is provided".(IDB 197)

The extent of the problem is shown by Table 3.8, which shows income from loan repayments in 15 institutions in 1978, compared with the total outstanding debt. In most cases loan repayments represented less than 10 per cent of total debt, and even in the case of the oldest, ICETEX it is only 14 per cent. Only in Brazil (APLUB), Honduras and Peru is it higher. One reason for this is the rapid escalation of educational credit in recent years, but another, of course, is the fact that all the student loan programs provide subsidies in the form of low interest sales, as well as long repayment periods and other generous repayment terms.

REPAYMENT TERMS

There are considerable differences in the length of repayment period of student loans in Latin America as well as in other repayment terms. These are summarised in Table 3.7. In some cases for example INCE in Argentina, the loan must be paid back in the same period of time as the student's borrowing period, while other programs, for example SACUEDO in Venezuela allow double the borrowing period, or three times in the Dominican Republic. Where a specific period of time is laid down, it ranges from 2 years in Peru (INABEC) and 4 years in some private programs in Mexico to 15 years in the case of Panama (IFARHU).

All the loan programs allow a grace period before repayment must commence, usually 6 months or a year. In some cases it is possible for borrowers to postpone repayments, or renegotiate repayment terms, if they are in financial difficulties, due to illness or unemployment, for example, but in no case is this automatic as in Sweden.

The method of making repayments varies. In most cases borrowers are required to pay through banks, or to send payments directly to the loan institutions, but in some cases deductions may be made from employees' salaries by either public or private employers, for example ICETEX is authorised to require this, in some cases.

Interest rates vary between countries, but are invariably below market rates of interest, and usually below the central bank discount rate. Dominguez (1973) found that in 1972 the interest rate on student loans in seven Latin American countries was about 2 per cent below central bank discount rates. A survey by IDB (1976) showed that in Jamaica, for example, the interest on student loans in 1972-3 was 6 per cent in 1972-73, when the central bank rate was 8.4 per cent and the annual rate of inflation was 10.8 per cent. Similarly, in Trinidad and Tobago interest on

TABLE 3.7

REPAYMENTS OF STUDENT LOANS AS A % OF TOTAL OUTSTANDING DEBTS, LATIN AMERICA, 1978

Bolivia (CIDEP)	8
Brazil (APLUB)	21
(Caixa Economica Federal)	1
Colombia (ICETEX)	14
Costa Rica (CONAPE)	0.2
Chile (Catholic University)	7
Ecuador (IECE)	8
El Salvador (Educredito)	8
Honduras (Educredito)	16
Jamaica (Students' Loan Bureau)	0.5
Mexico (Bank of Mexico)	12
Nicaragua (Educredito)	9
Panama (IFARHU)	6
Peru (INABEC)	48
Dominican Republic (FCE)	13
Venezuela (Educredito)	9
(SACUEDO)	2

Source: As Table 3.4

TABLE 3.8

REPAYMENT TERMS OF STUDENT LOANS, LATIN AMERICA 1978

	Interest (1) During Study	Interest (2) During Repayment	Length of Repayment	Grace Period
Argentina	Linked to cost of living and Bank Rate.		Same as borrowing	12 months
Bolivia	5%	5-15%	Max. 10 years.	3 months
Brazil (APLUB)	5%	10%	Same as borrowing	6-12 months
(Caixa Economica Federal)	12%+	12%+	variable	12 months
Colombia (ICETEX)	3-14%	6-16%	variable	3-6 months
Costa Rica	6-8%	6-8%	?	2-6 months
Chile (Catholic University)	Linked to cost of living		6 years	12 months
Ecuador	variable		6 years	variable
Honduras	8%	8%	8 years	3-6 months
Jamaica	6%	6%	9 years	12 months
Mexico (Bank of Mexico)	-	8.5-12%	7 years	12 months
Nicaragua	3%	6%	?	12 months
Panama	-	5%	15 years	?
Dominican Republic	12%	12%	3 x borrowing	variable
Venezuela (Educredito)	8%		variable	6 months
(SACUEDO)	3-8%	3-8%	2 x borrowing	6-12 months

Source: As Table 3.4

student loans was 5 per cent when bank rate averaged 8.2 per cent and inflation 12 pr cent.

Thus, the real rate of interest on student loans was negative, and student borrowers were receiving a substantial subsidy. As already shown in Table 1.2, Rogers calculated that this subsidy represented between 14 and 31 per cent of the value of the loan in Honduras, Panama and Mexico if the real interest rate in the economy was 8 per cent and between 39 and 61 per cent if the real interest rate were 16 per cent. (Rogers February 1972). In other words, according to this calculation about a quarter to a half of each loan is in fact a grant.

Since these estimates were made, both inflation and interest rates have risen markedly in Latin America. Interest rates on student loans have also risen, but are still well below market rates. In 1978, Panama (IFARHU), Nicaragua (Educredito) and Jamaica were still charging 5 or 6 per cent, but Mexico (Bank of Mexico), Honduras (Educredito) charged 8 per cent and ICETEX charged between 6 and 16 per cent, according to the length of repayment period.

In Chile, the amount to be repaid was linked with the consumer price index, as was the case in Sweden until 1975. Several countries charge higher rates of interest to defaulters, and Ecuador and Venezuela (SACUEDO) provide an incentive to borrowers to repay their loans quickly, by charging lower interest in such cases.

Most loan programs require borrowers to provide a personal guarantee. In some cases borrowers must promise to work in a particular occupation, or region, after completing their studies, and those who get a loan for study abroad must promise to return to work in their own country. For example, the Student Loan Fund run in Dominica, with assistance from the Caribbean Development Bank states "If the applicant is in the public service or teaching service, he must, after completing his studies undertake to work at least five years in such service, if the course of study is for a period of one year or more. In all other cases, the applicant must undertake to work, after completing his studies for at least three years in any of the less developed member states of the bank". (Dominica Agricultural and Industrial Development Bank).

THE COST OF ADMINISTERING STUDENT LOANS

There is very little information about the costs of administering student loans in Latin America. The only study to examine this question in detail is Herrick et al. (1974) which concludes:

> "The recent experience of several institutions shows a range of from 12 to 23 per cent for strictly administrative costs expressed as a percentage of total annual outlay. It seems reasonable to expect, however, that good management in an established institution can keep these costs down to 10 to 15 per cent".
>
> (Herrick et al. 1974, p.27)

This study gives various examples of operating and administrative costs which suggest that several institutions spend about 12 per cent of their total expenditure on administrative costs. ICETEX of Colombia and INCE of Argentina both spent about 12 per cent of their total 1972 expenditure on administration and Educredito in Honuras spent 12 per cent in 1971, but incurred extra expenditure in 1972 which increased the percentage to 17 per cent, and similarly, in Ecuador, IECE incurred high start-up costs, but projected 12 per cent by 1977. (Herrick et al. 1974) However, it was pointed out that administrative costs tend to be proportionately higher for growing institutions, and several countries predict a fall in administrative costs due to economies of scale.

In the case of a recent project evaluation by AID of a loan to the Fundacion de Credito Educativo (FCE) in the Dominican Republic, the assumption was made that the costs of administering student loans would be DR$80 a year, which is about 5 to 8 per cent of the average loan which will be made available, of $1,000 to $1,500 per student. The project assessment suggests that this figure will not vary with the size of a loan, nor with the total number of loans: "It may be that there are certain fixed costs (space rented or top management time) which do not increase with the size of the portfolio. However, it appears that most of FCE's costs are incurred in the physical processing of papers which are probably directly proportionate to the number of loans". (AID 1981, p.67)

The costs of administration depend very largely on the costs of collection and critics of student loans argue that the high costs of debt collection will drastically reduce the potential of student loans as a cost recovery mechanism. The cost of collection depend, very largely on the rate of default on student loans.

DEFAULT ON STUDENT LOANS

Because, as we have already seen, in Table 3.5, the proportion of student loans that have not yet become due for repayment is so high in many countries it is difficult to find reliable evidence on the extent of default in Latin America. Many individuals, particularly opponents of loans, refer to high rates of default, and some countries have experienced high default rates, but this is by no means a universal problem.

A review of IDB experience with loans to educational credit institutions suggest that the problem of defaults has proved serious in some Caribbean countries, (Ibacache 1978); the report quotes figures for Trinidad and Tobago which show that 67 per cent of the borrowers who had begun to repay their loans were late in their installments, and claims that the rate of defaults had fallen in Jamaica, but had previously been 50 per cent.

On the basis of this experience IDB now requires educational credit institutions to limit repayment installments to no more than 10 per cent of a borrowers' earnings, in the belief that this is the maximum feasible level of installments, any higher leading inevitably to default. This figure of 10 per cent of earnings is widely quoted as being the maximum level of repayments that should be demanded. Dominguez (1973) discusses the question of the maximum level of repayments at some length. He quotes American students who regard 4 per cent of income as the maximum they would be able to pay, but suggests "Students in developing countries, perhaps ought to be willing to accept a higher percentage" (Domingez 1973, p.145). On the other hand he regards 15 per cent as clearly unacceptable and supports Daniere (1964) in his belief that about 6.4 per cent of gross income or 7.5 per cent of disposable income (after tax and other legal deductions) represents "a socially acceptable ceiling".

Herrick et al (1974) examined default rates in Latin America and found considerable variety. In the case of Colombia, the study reports that ICETEX had an average 5 per cent annual loss, due to defaults between 1953 and 1968 and concludes "Considering the length of experience, history of good management and breadth of program of ICETEX this example illustrates probably the lowest rate of loss that can be expected. A rate of 10 per cent might not be unreasonable for any institution". (Herrick et.al. 1974, p.31)

Other examples quoted in this study are Honduras where the collection experience of Educredito is described as good "and it has been found that lower-income students have the better repayment records". On the other hand, the study quotes FCE, in the Dominican Republic as an example of an institution with severe collection problems. "FCE took over the portfolio of a predecessor organization, sponsored by the government, which had a very poor record of collection and had not succeeded in persuading recipients of credit that loans were indeed expected to be paid back. FCE believes that it has created some change in attitude. Borrowers on the whole understand the concept of an education loan, and the majority of them are making payments, though not necessarily on schedule. Collection of payments due, however, remains a pressing current problem for FCE."

(Herrick et al. 1974, p.29)

However, more recently, the AID report on the Dominican republic looked at default rates and found they varied by type of institution. The report quotes FCE as saying there is "generally no problem" in recovering loans from graduates of certain secondary technical schools, whereas in the case of another, loan defaults are over 50 per cent.

The report concludes "Loan defaults occur almost exclusively among students who leave school before they have finished their course work for a degree" (AID 1981, p.40).

This shows clearly that evidence of high default rates often indicates some other, underlying problem, such as high rates of wastage and drop-out. There is also a problem of how default rates should be measured. Some figures refer to the proportion of borrowers who are late in repaying their loans, others refer to the proportion of outstanding debt that is in arrears. Table 3.9 shows the proportion of debt that has already reached repayment stage but is in arrears. This varies from under 1 per cent in Costa Rica (CONAPE) to 30 per cent in Venezuela (Educredito). However the loan scheme in Costa Rica is so new that it is impossible to estimate default accurately yet.

Herrick et al. refer to other problems in measuring and comparing default rates, for example "in some countries the normal practice is to pay debts within 30 days whereas in others 60 or 90 days may be quite acceptable". This study does suggest that "it seems to be a common experience for education credit institutions to find that the first year

TABLE 3.9

% OF DEBTS DUE FOR REPAYMENT IN ARREARS OR DEFUALT

LATIN AMERICA, 1978

Brazil (APLUB)	2
Colombia (ICETEX)	11
Costa Rica (CONAPE)	0.5
Ecuador (IECE)	19
Honduras (Educredito)	9
Jamaica (Students' Loan Bureau)	7
Mexico (Bank of Mexico)	5
Peru (INABEC)	22
Venezuela (Educredito)	30
(SACUEDO)	8

Source: As Table 3.4

or two of the authorization period is the most difficult in terms of collection".

This suggests that it would be much better if Latin American countries, like Sweden, distinguished between those who had postponed repayment, perhaps because of difficulties in finding a first job, when the "grace period" was insufficient (only 3-6 months in some countries) and those who refused to repay, or could not repay at all. To classify both those who missed paying an installment for a month or two in the early period of amortization and those who genuinely cannot or will not repay as "defaulters" is to confuse the issue. The evidence from Latin America does not suggest that default is an insoluable problem, but that it requires more research.

SECTION IV

STUDENT LOANS IN OTHER DEVELOPING COUNTRIES

Student loans are not found so extensively in other regions, but there are a number of small programs in Asia and Africa, a long established program in Israel, and there was a short-lived experiment in Ghana from which some interesting lessons can be learned. This section does not attempt a comprehensive survey of all Developing countries where loans are to be found, but gives details of the main programs in developing countries that have been discussed in the literature. The first program to be described is one of the most interesting, since it is quoted as an experiment that failed, although it has also been described as "one of the more imaginative programs in the field of financing higher education in Africa" (Williams 1974, p.339).

GHANA

The student loan scheme in Ghana was short-lived; it was introduced in June 1971, but abandoned in October 1972, after only a year because of the overthrow of the government that had introduced it and the opposition of the new Head of State to the idea of student loans. Although it cannot be counted a success, since its unpopularity with students was one major cause of its abolition, there are nevertheless some interesting lessons for other developing countries both in the experience itself and in the fierce debate that surrounded the introduction and abolition of the program. Many of these lessons are explored in an interesting description of the whole episode by a co-opted member of the Committee which recommended the introduction of student loans in Ghana, Peter Williams, who was at the time Ford Foundation Advisor to the Ministry of Education. (Williams 1974)

The introduction of a student loan scheme in Ghana was first suggested in 1968 by a committee which recommended that the government should no longer provide full scholarships to all university students but provide three types of financial aid;

a) scholarships for students of outstanding merit.

b) bursaries for those on "manpower-priority courses"

c) interest free loans for other students.

Before introducing such a scheme the government appointed another committee, under Mr. Dowuona to examine the case for student loans and produce detailed proposals. At that time every Ghanaian who won a place on an undergraduate, dipolma, or certificate course was granted a "scholarship" representing full tuition fees, board and lodgings. This was far more generous than the system prevailing in secondary education, where pupils were expected to pay their own board and lodgings expenses, and in the case of sixth-form pupils they were also expected to buy books and stationery. The fortunate university student, on the other hand, received a scholarship to cover all out of pocket expenses, as well as free tuition and board and lodgings. In 1968-69, the total cost of each university student, according to the Dowuona Committee was about NC3,000, compared with only NC200 per secondary school pupil and only cC20 for each primary school pupil. Thus, on grounds of social equity it was argued that the government should "redress the imbalance in expediture on the various sections of the system "(Ghana: Government Statement 1970) by recovering part of the cost of higher ducation by means of fees for board and lodgings, with loans for students who could not afford the new fees.

In the Parliamentary debate that accompanied the introduction of student loans, the Prime Minister pointed out that "Under present arrangements, the people who get higher up the education ladder, even though their earning capacity is greatly increased, are subsidised to a greater extent than those lower down. It means that the tax-payer pays more for those who are receiving higher education". (Ghana: Parliamentary Debates 1971).

The arguments for loans was thus linked with the question of fees for maintenance,(though not for tuition) and the two measures must be seen together, as part of the same strategy of reducing the financial burden of higher education by recovering part of the costs from those who, it was argued, would benefit substantially from their university education.

The Committee argued that it was necessary and desirable to reduce the financial burden of higher education and introduce loans because:

1) The level of subsidy involved in the scholarships had been introduced as a "short term measure" to overcome manpower shortages, and so high a subsidy was no longer necessary, since the number of university students had already grown dramatically from just over 300 in 1951 to 5,000 in 1969;

2) Loan repayments would eventually yield savings to the government budget of NC2.5 million, just over 15 per cent of university costs, which could be redistributed among lower levels of education and thus the funds saved could help achieve universal primary education.

3) Social justice demanded that the beneficiaries of higher education should contribute something directly to the public cost of universities. Under the terms of the loan scheme, the "graduate would be required to repay each year an amount equal to less than 20 per cent of the additional income society has made it possible for him to earn through his university training". (Ghana: Government Committee, 1970).

The proposal, which was accepted by the government, was that students should pay fees of NC500 p.a. for board and lodgings, but should receive loans which must be repaid over 12 years, by means of monthly deductions from salary. The statement by the Government of Ghana, explaining and justifying the new student loan scheme makes it clear that students would still receive free tuition, that all students would be eligible for loans, regardless of income and there would be scholarships and grants, awarded partly on grounds of manpower priorities, available to about 10 per cent of new entrants. No interest would be charged, although a "service charge" of 1 per cent would be levied, after a grace period of four years.

Thus, the system of loans was far more generous than that in any Latin American country; nevertheless it was bitterly attacked by students (despite the fact that students representatives on the Dowuona Committee had voted for a loan scheme) and by others, who argued that if it was necessary to recover part of the costs of higher education then this should be done by means of a compulsory graduate tax, which would affect those who had already benefitted from free university education, and not impose an unfair burden on new students. For example Aidam argued strongly "we should not become the nation that only bequeathes to its future generations debts and financial obligations. We should be the kind of nation that, aware of its dire problems, calls upon those who have been around while the problems were being created to face the music" (Aidam 1971, p.10). His specific proposal was a flat rate "Special University Education Tax" for all graduates.

Others argued that if it was necessary to make savings this could be done by improving university efficiency, and reducing extravagance rather than charging fees and introducing loans. Nevertheless the loan scheme was introduced, and Peter Williams points out that "the alleged deterrent effects of student loans on university entry did not appear to materialise. In the year the loans scheme was introduced the number admitted to Ghanaian universities for the first degree courses rose substantially, reversing a declining trend since 1967" (Williams 1974, p.343).

However, political events overtook the student loan scheme. The government that had introduced loans was overthrown in 1971. The leader of the new government announced that "As a matter of principle, I am opposed to the student loans scheme and it is my intention as soon as practicable, steps should be taken to abolish it. I believe faithfully that every citizen of the land has an inalienable right to free education" (Acheampong 1972).

Thus, the system of fees and loans was withdrawn after only a year, and all that remains of a loan scheme in Ghana is a small loan, administered by the banks to enable students to buy essential equipment. Williams argues that it is "plausible to explain the abandonment of the scheme in political terms". In other words, the new government needed to win support, and "it was the unrelenting opposition by students to the scheme which caused the (new government) to kill it". (Williams 1974, p339,343). As other commentators have made clear, students are a powerful political force in Ghana, as elsewhere in Africa. Finally, Williams concludes that the Ghana Student Loan Scheme was an accidental victim of the political circumstance of the change of governments with abolition of the scheme being a useful tactical weapon for the new government in the early days". (Williams 1974, p.342).

However, Williams draws some valuable lessons from this experience about the political acceptability of student loans, and about their feasibility in an African context. He argues that the first mistake was that no real attempt was made to mobilise public opinion. "The scheme was introduced at short notice, and no sustained campaign of public explanation was launched". Secondly, he argues that more should have been done to reduce costs of university education in other ways, so that students did not have "a real feeling of resentment at being made the scapegoats of the country's failure to control higher education costs". He does not argue that this would have been an alternative to introducing fees and loans, since he believes that "reduction of costs and charges are essentially complementary rather than conflicting approaches to the financial problem". However, he concludes "Those who preach austerity to students should be prepared to practise it themselves. Student loans are not a soft option for African governments, an easy alternative to difficult policies. They can usefully contribute to the improvement of higher education in Africa and to fairer African societies. But if they are to be fully accepted they must be part of a program of common endeavour with equality of sacrifice by leaders as well as led" (Williams 1974, pp. 341-343).

The Ghana experience is interesting because it is one of the only examples of a government introducing loans, together with fees, as a way of reducing the costs of higher education. As such, Williams welcomes it as "a courageous departure in the field of student loans. Loan programs elsewhere in the world have tended to lighten the financial contribution of students and their parents to the costs of higher education. Ghana was asking them to pay more" (Williams 1974, p. 345).

The Ghana Scheme was too short-lived to show whether it would have been possible to put into effect and whether collection problems and defaults would have nullified any potential savings. However, it was clear that the scheme could never have been completely self-financing, since no interest was to be charged, at least initially. In fact, the Committee's estimate that eventually NC2.5 million could be saved was probably optimistic, and greater savings could have been made if the terms of the loans had been less generous. However, given the students' opposition to even a highly subsidised loans scheme, it would be difficult to argue that the government should have taken a harsher line.

The government of Ghana was, of course, well aware that there would be no immediate savings from the introduction of the loans scheme, and sought to overcome this problem by means of a loan from the World Bank, to finance a number of projects, including the introduction of the loans scheme. The government's arguments for the IBRD loan was that it had an immediate need for resources for other sectors of education, that although the introduction of fees and loans would eventually yield substantial savings, it would be at least 15 years before the full savings could be realised, because of the long repayment period. A World Bank Loan would, therefore, have enabled the government of Ghana to anticipate the expected savings.

At that time, the IDB and AID had helped finance student loan projects in LDC's but the World Bank had not done so, although it was seriously considering the potential of loans as a way of recovering part of the costs of higher education and in fact in 1971 it began a research project on the student loan program in Colombia, (Jallade 1974). It was no doubt felt that it would be better to await the results of that study before the World Bank initiated lending to student loan institutions. It was also suggested that there were flaws in the student loan program as conceived by the government. For example, the repayment terms had been criticised by various observers, and, as the students themselves argued, it would be possible to reduce the high costs of university education in other ways. Finally it has been suggested that the scheme was not feasible since the capital needed to have made the scheme self-financing would have exceeded 1% of Ghana's GNP (Dominguez 1976). For a variety of reasons, therefore, World Bank assistance for the introduction of a loan program in Ghana was not forthcoming.

Subsequent events may suggest that with or without such assistance the project was already doomed. Williams has shown that the scheme was deeply opposed by students, and later experience suggests that the co-operation of students may be a pre-requisite for the successful launching of a student loam program. However, it would be unfortunate if this experience were used as evidence that loan schemes are not feasible in Africa. Williams, for example, shows that the introduction of loans did not reduce the number of students who enrolled in universities in 1971, and he also says that student loans "seemed to have been accepted by the public at large and even student opposition was less vocal once the scheme was in operaton....Only time could have demonstrated that the students loan scheme would not impair....access for the poorest, but the necessary time was not vouchsafed" (Williams 1974, p.343).

Far from proving that student loan schemes would not work in Africa, the short-lived experiment in Ghana demonstrates the need for such an innovation in financing to be accompanied by powerful publicity and to be seen as part of a general policy of reducing the high costs of university education. When the student loan scheme was withdrawn, the student organisation suggested alternative ways of saving government funds in higher education, mainly consisting of attempts to "reduce waste". If such measures had preceded the introduction of loans they would not have been regarded as an alternative, for as Williams emphasises in his assessment of the Ghana experiment, reductions in costs and the introduction of fees plus loans are essentially complementary, rather than conflicting solutions to the financing problem.

LOAN SCHEMES IN OTHER AFRICAN COUNTRIES

The Dowuona Committee in Ghana argued that though a loans scheme was novel in Ghana, similar schemes were in operation in other countries, but the only African country mentioned was Tanzania, where a limited scheme, existed. It is still a small scheme, covering only a proportion of students' living expenses, but a recent Presidential Education Commission, reporting on Tanzanian education needs to the year 2000 has suggested that in future university students should pay their own living expenses and buy books and materials. If this were to be implemented an expanded loan scheme might be called for.

In Nigeria there was a small Federal government loan scheme, together with a system of tuition fees plus grants, but this system was fundamentally changed in 1977/8, when tuition fees were abolished, and responsibility for grants and loans was transferred from the Federal government to the States. Some States still have a small loan scheme but in general loans are available only for students who are studying abroad, and even then they are regarded as a supplementary source of funds for those who have already begun a course of higher education abroad but encountered financial difficulties.

A recent article on the costs and benefits of university education in Nigeria (Mbanefoh 1981) suggests that the loan scheme which was operated by the Nigerian Students Loan Board experienced problems, particularly with default:
"The problem of repayment is administrative but crucial, as it has unfortunately dampened the enthusiasm of Government about the students loan program, in spite of the assertions of the current Nigerian Students Loans Board that there is no evidence in its records to indicate that the number of defaulters is anything but minimal. No fresh awards have been made to students in Nigerian Institutions of Higher Learning since 1977/78 academic session, and the outstanding loan was reported to have stood close to 14 million by 1978. Shifting responsibility for the student loan scheme to lower levels of government, as the Federal Government is curently doing would probably not solve the problem, since the former are very likely to lack the necessary funds with which to execute the program" (Mbanefoh 1981, p 240).

However, Mbanefoh believes that a loan scheme should be reintroduced in Nigeria, and argues that the private rate of return is sufficiently high to provide an incentive to students to invest in higher education, even if they paid the full cost of tuiton as well as board and lodging. However, since many students could not afford to finance this out of family income, he recommends a public student loan program, but believes that eligibility for loans, and the amount of loan provided, should depend on financial need and family income. The way a means-tested student loan might work in Nigeria is shown in Figure 4.1, where Mbanefoh shows that students with family incomes of less than N 2,000 would require a maximum loan, but those with higher incomes would receive smaller loans until those with incomes above N 8,000 would not be eligible for a loan.

The argument for such a scheme, according to Mbanefoh is that "governmental resources are not yet such that would make university education free to all those who desire it. In the present circumstance, a rationing device for allocating the limited available spaces is called for". He believes that tuition fees, combined with loans, would perform this function efficiently and equitably. However, there is no discussion of the political acceptability of such a scheme in Nigeria, even though he admits that tuition fees were abolished in 1977/8 because "university students revolted against their share of the cost of their education, on the grounds that it was too high" (Mbanefoh 1981, p. 232).

Another country where there is a small loan scheme, but where much greater reliance on student loans has been proposed is Kenya. Both Rogers (February 1971 and January 1972) and Fields (in Court and Ghai 1974) recommend a loan scheme where borrowers repay a fixed proportion of their income each year, and argue that even if students were to pay the full costs of their university educaton, under a loan scheme, they would still enjoy a substantial private rate of return.

Rogers estimated rates of return in Kenya using 1968 salary

FIGURE 4.1

PROPOSED LOAN SCHEME FOR NIGERIAN STUDENTS:
LOAN REQUIREMENTS BY STUDENTS BASED ON ABILITY TO PAY

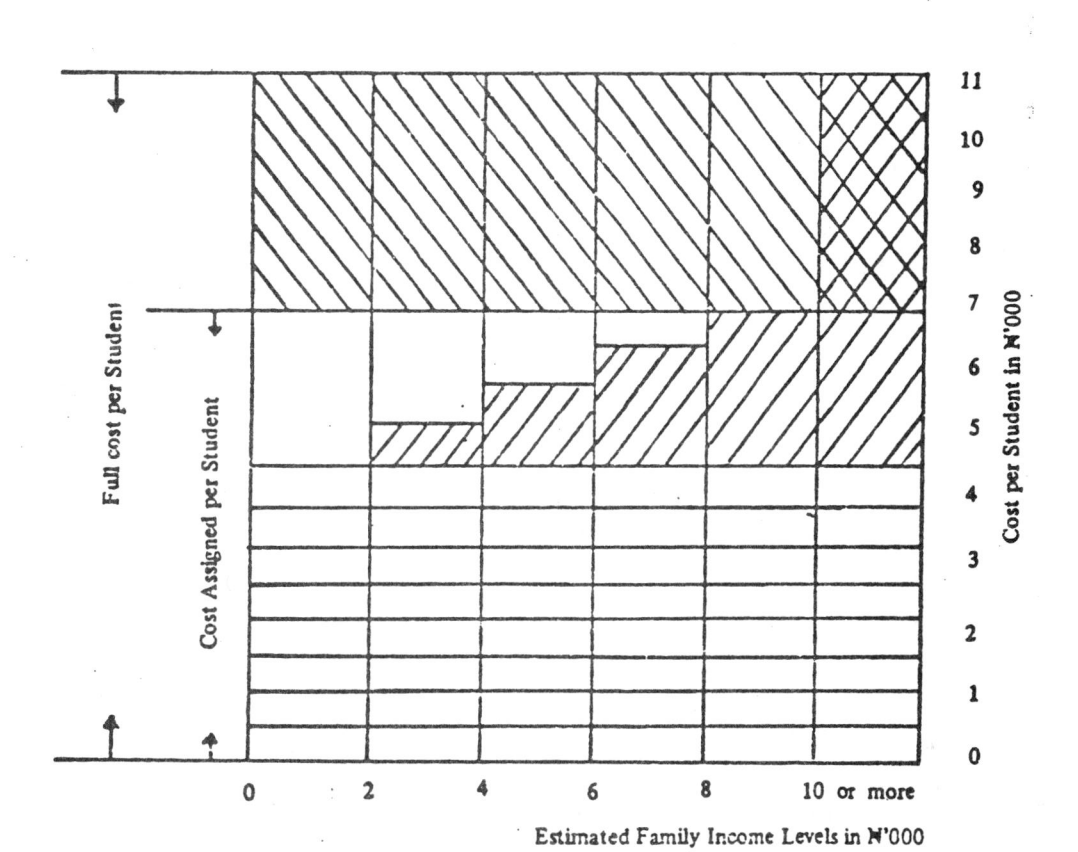

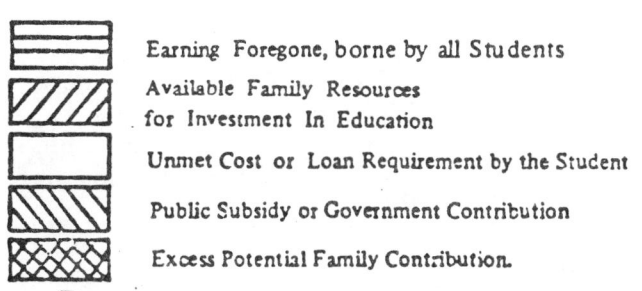

Legend:
- Earning Foregone, borne by all Students
- Available Family Resources for Investment In Education
- Unmet Cost or Loan Requirement by the Student
- Public Subsidy or Government Contribution
- Excess Potential Family Contribution.

The excess potential family contribution portion for the ₦10,000 or more income group indicates the costs not assigned to the student which could have been borne by the family, had such demands been made on it. It, therefore, represents an **excess investible** fund to the family which could be diverted to other purposes.

Source: Mbanefoh 1981, p.239

scales and the private costs of education which were very low, since students received free tuition, books, room and board, and a small cash grant to cover clothing and other living expenses. He estimated private rates of return of over 20 per cent for teacher training and university graduates, and then recalculated the rates of return for three alternative financing systems:-

1) "pay-as-you-go" - i.e. students paid the full costs of their education.

2) "fixed-amount" loans, to cover full-costs, i.e. a conventional loan where borrowers repay the full costs of their education by regular installments;

3) "percentage of earnings" loan, i.e. an income-contingent loan to cover the full costs of tuition plus board.

These calculations show that private rates of return under the loan schemes would still be about 17 per cent and Rogers proposed an income-contingent loan scheme, on the grounds that this would generate very substantial revenue for the government, and that "the resources supporting one university student for a year could support 158 primary school students for that period (Rogers January 1972, p.259). Table 4.1 shows the estimates of the revenue that would be generated by alternative loan schemes, including:-

1) fixed repayment, with zero or 7 per cent interest, for a 10 year, 20-year of lifetime repayment period.

2) income-contingent (percentage of income) with zero or 7 per cent interst and 10, 20-year or life-time repayment.

This table shows that if interest of 7 per cent were charged, and borrowers had to repay loans in 10 years, the scheme (assuming a 7.5 per cent default rate) could, by the fifteenth year of the scheme, generate revenue one and half times the total reccurrent cost of universities (£5,273.000, compared with £3,396,000) and even if the loans were interest-free, and spread over a whole life-time, the repayments would still represent a third of total costs by the fifteenth year (£1,133.00, compared with £3,396.000). However, these calculations are now out of date.

By the time Fields (1974) calculated rates of return, using 1971 salary scales the private rate of return had substantially increased, since the government had increased civil service salary scales for graduates by 50 per cent. This meant that with the existing levels of subsidy university graduates enjoyed a private rate of return of over 30 per cent, and Field therefore reinforced Rogers' argument for an income-contingent loan scheme, covering the full costs of educaton. He argued that such a scheme would have the following advantages over the existing, full-subsidy system:

a) Less redistribution of income from poor to rich and from tax-payers to graduates and their families;

TABLE 4.1

ESTIMATED REVENUE FROM ALTERNATE LOAN PROGRAMS FOR UNIVERSITY STUDENTS

KENYA, 1971/2 - 1985/6

Type of Loan:	Fixed Sum						% of Income		
Repayment Period:	10 Year		20 Year		Lifetime		Lifetime		Total Recurrent Cost of University
Interest Rate:	0%	7%	0%	7%	0%	7%	0%	7%	

Tuition, Room, and Board (£1,431)

Annual Payment:	£143	£204	£72	£135	£42	£90	2.5%	6.0%	

(£1,000)

1971/72	67	94	33	63	20	41	11	28	-
1975/76	499	711	251	471	147	313	92	229	-
1980/81	1,129	1,611	569	1,067	332	710	232	575	-
1985/86	1,356	1,947	938	1,759	549	1,174	418	1,042	-
1971/72 through 1985/86	12,160	17,347	6,807	12,763	3,978	8,501	2,803	6,968	-

Full Cost (£3,876)

Annual Payment	£387	£552	£195	£366	£114	£243	6.7%	16 1/4%	

(£1,000)

1971/72	181	255	89	170	53	112	29	75	2,093
1975/76	1,352	1,926	680	1,276	397	847	248	621	2,469
1980/81	3,058	4,363	1,541	2,890	900	1,924	628	1,557	2,922
1985/86	3,697	5,273	2,541	4,764	1,486	3,179	1,133	2,823	3,396
1971/72 through 1985/86	32,935	46,985	18,437	34,569	10,776	23,026	7,593	18,874	44,306

A 7.5 per cent default rate assumed.
A Kenya £ is equal to $2.80

Source: Rogers, February 1971, p.25

b) More rapid economic growth in the longer run;

c) Lower private rates of return to investment in education and thus less demand for education and less pressure on the educational system at all levels to expand;

d) More serious and committed students and workers who are aware of the debt owed their government;

e) An incentive for students to seek greater efficiency in the schools, since lower average costs would result in lower repayment rates. It would also have advantages over a fixed-amount loan scheme:

f) No disincentive effect on those who might choose to enter low-paying but worthy occupations;

g) A pooling of risks, so that the individual is not liable for a fixed amount in the event of personal disaster;

h) Constancy of payment in real terms (an advantage to the Government).
(Fields 1974, p.195)

Both Rogers and Fields believed that an income-contingent loan scheme would be feasible in Kenya, even though the small scale loan scheme that did exist, was not regarded as a success. Rogers argued that,

"Many have suggested that loans for education are impossible to collect in developing countries. What I am suggesting is that if the right program is instituted with sufficient incentives and sanctions, repayment will not be politically or socially impracticable....

The Kenyan Government already has a loan program for financing university education which has been small and repayments have been slow. I would suggest that there is a casual relationship here. There is a great feeling that the program is unfair because only a small minority of all those receiving higher education have to pay for it. It would appear that a program encompassing all students would have a much better chance of success in collecting the money due and receiving popular support.
(Rogers, February 1971, p.26)

Similarily, Fields argues that:-

"If a loan program is politically feasible, I see no reason why the inclusion of interest charges would not also be. The initial unpopularity is unquestionable, particularly among current or prospective recipients of higher education, whose tax burdens would as much as double. But public support might well be enlisted if the people are informed that implementation of the proposed scheme would free budgetary resources which, in the absence of other financial constraints, would allow primary school fees to be eliminated. Alternatively, Kenya could educate 300,000 more primary students a year or have 2,000 new hospital beds or 4,000 kilometres of new roads. Yet higher education would

>continue to be a highly lucrative and rewarding personal investment. The charges and payments could readily be administered by the Tax Department, particularly if the tax system is streamlined to alleviate the double income taxation which now exists."
>
>(Fields 1974, p.195)

The problem is that of the political unpopularity of removing what is agreed, by all observers, to be a very substantial subsidy for a small, priveleged elite. Rogers asks "Why have such programs not sprung up all over the globe? First and foremost there is the politcal cost. University students are an elite in Developing countries and they know it, and are treated as such. Anything that might adversely affect their interests is strenuously fought". (Rogers, February 1971, p.26).

Since this was written the Kenyan government has inroduced a new loan scheme, to cover students' living expenses. Between 1974, when the scheme was introduced, and 1981, a total of K£20 million has been provided to students in the form of loans. Graduates must begin to repay their loans after a grace period of two to four years, and the normal repayment period is about 7 or 8 years, with interest charged at 2 per cent.

The experience with collecting loan repayments has been disappointing, and it is estimated that half of all students who should have begun to repay their loan by 1982 were late or in default; in several cases this was because students had dropped out of universities before completing their course, and the original regulations of the Student Loan Scheme made no provision for this. Another weakness of the original design of the University Loan Scheme was that no effective machinery was established to secure collection of loan repayments. It is recognised that the main problem is one of keeping records, when students or graduates change addresses frequently, and may change names. A recent attempt by the government to introduce a clause whereby parental land should be used as collateral for the loan provoked student demonstrations in 1981.

However, despite these problems, the Ministry of Education, which administers the scheme has announced its determination to secure repayment of outstanding loans and has made no plans to change the scheme, although there is currently a University of Nairobi Visiting and Inspection Committee which is reviewing the loan scheme, and will make recommendations for improving it.

The experience in Kenya, therefore, as in other African countries, shows that student loan schemes may face considerable problems. However, the goverment is attempting to solve these problems by improving collection mechanisms, rather than abandoning the loan scheme.

STUDENT LOANS IN ASIA

Student loans were introduced on a small scale in India, but have never been a major source of financing higher education, although the Planning Commission argued in 1966 that greater emphasis should be placed on loans, which "after a period of initial investment develop into a self-generating, self-perpetuating fund". (quoted in Azad 1975 p.209). However there has never been a comprehensive loan program in India, but a number of proposals have been made for example, Azad, after reviewing all the arguments against loans, including the "difficulties of administering a loan programe on such a large scale as the ever-expanding enrolments in India will necessitate", nevertheless, argues that it is a question of "selecting the lesser evil", and recommends a loan scheme, on the grounds that the country could not afford grants for all those who "face the grim prospect of being denied higher education for want of adequate financial support". He argues that "It may be stated that in India, for quite some time, a loan program will have a limited operational validity. In view of the financial constraints, however, it will be necessary to take recourse to this sytem (Azad, 1975 p 211-2).

Azad suggests that because of the size of India, with a student population of about 3.5 million at the university stage and over 4,000 colleges and 100 universities, a centralised loan scheme would be impossible to administer, but believes that a decentralised system, involving state governments and universities would be possible.

The fact that a small-scale loan scheme was in operation in India was one factor which persuaded the People's Bank in Sri Lanka to establish a loan program "with a view to easing the indebtedness of the people and to accelerate the development of the country." The University Loan Scheme of the People's Bank was set up in 1964, and in 1978 an assessment was carried out for the Bank by Hewagama which provides very useful information about the program and its success. (Hewagama 1978).

The loans are provided by the People's Bank at 4 per cent interest, and graduates are expected to start repaying as soon as they have a job. A sample of about 1,000 students and past borrowers was questioned, and this provided valuable information about the income level and subsequent employment of borrowers. The loan scheme is clearly used by low income families. More than half the sample stated that their families were not income-tax payers, and more than a third had very low incomes, although the Bank did not accept the income figures as "totally correct" and in any case this question had a very low response rate.

The survey shows that a high proportion of borrowers were employed at the time of the survey, but many of these had been unemployed for long periods after graduation. Table 4.2 shows that even among those who were employed at the time of the survey (and 26 per cent of the sample were not) nearly 75 per cent had to wait over a year, after graduation, to obtain employment and nearly 30 per cent had to wait over 3 years.

This helps to explain the poor repayment record of the scheme. In 1978 loan repayments amounted to only 12 per cent of the total (Rs 38 million) that had been lent to students. The problem of unemployment, which is common in so many developing countries, and the fact that so many graduates had to wait long periods before finding a job suggests that the "grace period" allowed in many loan schemes is insufficient. Nevertheless, Hewagama commented:

> "It would not be correct to conclude that the loan scheme was a failure. It is possible that a more practical system of loan recoveries could be worked out. There were several positive

TABLE 4.2

PROPORTION OF BORROWERS WHO HAD BEEN UNEMPLOYED, IN SRI LANKA, 1978, BY LENGTH OF UNEMPLOYMENT

Year of Entry to University	1969	1970	1973	1976	Total	%
Below 1 year	30	29	17	01	77	25.67
1 – 2 years	09	09	29	–	47	15.66
2 – 3 years	16	25	24	–	65	21.67
3 – 4 years	19	13	02	–	34	11.33
4 – 5 years	13	07	–	–	20	6.66
Above 5 years	18	02	01	–	21	12.00
Total	109	88	97	06	300	100.00

Source: Hewagama 1978

Note The figures do not add to 100%. There are 7 per cent unaccounted for, but the table does not explain whether this is due to non-response, or some other reason.

features about this scheme, most important of all being that most of these students may never have completed their University course if the Banks had not made available to them such a facility. There is therefore a social obligation on the part of the Banks to keep this scheme going. But as bankers, procedures would have to be tightened up by the institution to ensure ultimate recovery of these funds".

Thus, despite the problems, Hewagama concludes: "We are of the opinion that necessary steps should be taken to improve the recoveries and the scheme should be continued". The report identifies various measures that could improve collection:-

- a) employers should deduct loan repayments at source, and the law should make this compulsory;

- b) there should be a campaign, accompanied by mass publicity, to punish defaulters.

- c) Employers should be required to obtain a statement of debts before employing graduates.

The final conclusion of the study however is:-

"We strongly recommend that the University Loan Scheme should be continued as it has benefits for both students and the bank and also for the country and the economy as a whole in the long run".
(Hewagama 1978)

This conclusion is interesting because it is not the conclusion of a government but of a study examining the scheme from the point of view of a commercial bank, which is concerned with financial reality, rather than arguments for public subsidy. Commercial banks also operate a student loan scheme in Pakistan, where the banks are nationalized. This is the Qarz-e-Hasna scheme, launched in 1980-1, to replace a Federal Government Students Loan Scheme introduced in 1974. The government provided half the finance for this scheme, and the commercial banks provided the other half. The regulations of the new Qarz-e-Hasna scheme state that "The actual operation of the Federal Government Students Loan Scheme during the last 6 years, and its evaluation has brought to light its various shortcomings and operational difficulties." No details are given of these shortcomings, except that the old scheme charged interest and "the heavy burden of the loan because of the interest element did not prove conducive to the achievement of the purpose of the scheme".

The Quarz-e-Hasna program provides interest-free loans for study in Pakistan or abroad, in scientific or technical subjects or medicine. The loans are means-tested, and may fall into three categories:

- a) comprehensive loan to cover all tuition and living costs.

- b) partial loan, to supplement a scholarship or other aid which is unsufficient.

- c) travel loan, to provide assistance for those who are

studying abroad.

The scheme will be administered by the five nationaized banks, under directions from the Pakistan Banking Council. Repayment normally starts after a grace period of 2 years, but unemployed graduates may have a longer grace period. The normal repayment period is 10 years.

The problem of "brain drain" is often mentioned as an obstacle to a student loan scheme in developing countries. The regulations of the Quarz-e-Hasna scheme state:-

> "The borrowing students will have to furnish a simple bond that after successful completion of the studies for which a loan has been granted to him, he would serve in Pakistan for at least till his loan is fully repaid. The Loanee Student would be provided with every opportunity to serve in Pakistan, and if such an opportunity offered to him is declined by him he would be liable to pay a penalty upto twice the amount of loan outstanding depending on his financial condition and repayment capacity. If the student fails to secure a suitable job in Pakistan within a reasonable time he will have the option of taking employment abroad, in which case he will be liable to pay only the original amount of the loan within the period originally agreed".
> (Qarz-e-Hasna Scheme Regulations).

The scheme is too recent to allow evaluation, but an evaluation committee will be set up, involving the Ministry of Finance, the Ministry of Education, the State Bank of Pakistan, the Pakistan Banking Council and the five nationalized banks.

Another very recent scheme is the Hong Kong Government student loan scheme set up in 1981 to provide loans for students studying in the UK, where overseas students must now pay full-cost fees. The purpose of this scheme is to "maintain reasonably high numbers in British universities", because of constitutional links between Hong Kong and the UK and because British qualifications are highly valued in Hong Kong. The loan committment for 1981-2 was $21.7 million and this was intended to provide loans for about 1000 students. By January 1982 over 1800 students had applied for loans, and over 1,000 were awarded. A report by the Hong Kong government in 1982 stated that "the loan scheme has slowed down the rate of decline but not arrested it".

However, the future of this scheme may be uncertain, since the Hong Kong government is at the moment engaged in negotiations with the British government, which would lead to Hong Kong students being charged the same fees as British students in return for a direct subsidy from the Hong Kong government.

STUDENT LOANS IN THE MIDDLE EAST

There is a small loan scheme in Egypt, but a survey carried out by I.I.E.P. (Sanyal et.al.1982) showed that only 5 per cent of the students questioned had received a government loan and about 2 per cent had received a non-government loan. The majority (nearly 80 per cent) relied on family support for their finance, but 18 per cent had a scholarship.

There is a long-established Student Loan scheme in Israel. The Fund was set up in 1964 to give students financial help with tuition fees. Higher education is not free in Israel, although fees are not intended to cover full costs; fees are 25 per cent higher for students whose fees are paid by their employer.

The Student Loan Fund is financed partly by the government and partly by six major banks. According to the budget of the Fund for 1980-1, the banks were expected to provide 50 per cent of the income of the Fund, the government 40 per cent and loan repayments the remaining 10 per cent, but actual expenditure was less than planned, so the government contribution was less than 40 per cent. (Israel, Council for Higher Education 1982).

In 1977-8, over 6,000 loans were provided, which represented 12 per cent of the total student population. More than a third of these students were from disadvantaged families. In 1980-1 5,833 loans were awarded.

The loans are administered by the banks, on behalf of the Student Loan Fund. The loans have a low interest rate, but must be repaid within two years. Students must pay a small contribution to a Loan Insurance Fund which covers loans written off due to disability. Between 1964 and 1977 the Student Loan Fund awarded nearly 70,000 loans, and reported that repayment in arrears was only 4 per cent and loans in default or written off were negligible.

There is one very interesting feature of the Israeli scheme, which is unusual, if not unique. A student who is awarded a loan may opt for a grant of 35 per cent of the value of the loan instead of the loan. This figure presumably represents the subsidy which is provided for borrowers in the form of low interest rates. Calculations in other countries show that this subsidy varies from 25 to over 50 per cent in some Latin American programs, and is more than 50 per cent of the value of NDSLP loans in the USA. In Israel the subsidy is less, because of the short repayment period, but Israeli students have the choice, not usually granted to students in other countries, of receiving this subsidy as a grant or as a loan.

SECTION V

EVALUATION OF STUDENT LOANS IN DEVELOPING COUNTRIES

Earlier sections of this paper have quoted the conclusions of many student aid evaluations in developed countries, that loans are a feasible means of financing higher education, that they can provide long term savings of government funds, without imposing undue burdens on borrowers, provided that there are adequate safeguards for those with low incomes, that they are more flexible than a system of financing which relies exclusively on grants or scholarships, and that they are both more efficient, in terms of effects on motivation of students, and more equitable in terms of redistribution of income. This section summarises a number of evaluations of student loans in developing countries in terms of these same criteria:

1) feasibility

2) level of public expenditure and subsidy of higher education.

3) flexibility

4) efficiency

5) equity

In addition, since many developing countries are preoccupied with questions of manpower policy, we add:

6) contributions to the supply of trained manpower.

FEASIBILITY

The first conclusion from this summary of experience is that student loan schemes can operate successfully in developing countries, but that those who advocate loans as a means of financing higher education frequently underestimate the amount of capital that will be needed to make a loan program self-financing, and the political opposition to combining loans with fees in order to reduce the level of subsidy for students.

Of their feasibility, particularly in Latin America, there can be no doubt. The study by Herrick et al. (1974) for US AID concludes that:

> "The student loan movement in Latin America is growing steadily in size and influence. It is developing and enlarging sources of financing for education credit and is helping to create acceptance for the idea that students should undertake greater financial responsibility for their own education. Education credit institutions have played a substantial role in promoting a variety of support for students in post-secondary education. Their programs have enabled thousands of students of limited economic means to participate in higher education. They have helped to persuade governments and educational institutions that scholarships programs should be converted to loan programs, which

make far more efficient use of the financial resources granted to
students. The very existence of these institutions, which are
capable of objective administration of loans and scolarships, has
stimulated new sources of education grants and credits from
government ministries, municipal governments, private business,
interested individuals, and foreign donors".
(Herrick et al. 1974).

On the other hand, experience outside Latin America shows that
loan schemes are much more rare in other regions, and where they do exist,
in Africa or Asia, they tend to be small-scale schemes. There are a number
of reasons for this. In Africa, both Anglo-phone and Franco-phone, the
tradition of providing free tuition and generous scholarships is well
established, and it is politically much more difficult to remove
subsidies, once granted, than to offer new sources of finance for
students, as was done in many Latin American countries.

Another reason is that credit institutions are well-established
in Latin America for other purposes. This also seems to be important in
explaining the popularity of student loan schemes in Scandinavia. In a
country like Norway or Sweden, where government funds provide loans to
individuals for house purchase or for setting up small businesses, it is
simply a logical extension of this to provide loans for students. A study
of the possibilities for using local community resources to support
education (Kulakow et.al. 1978) quotes the example of credit union self-
financing projects for agricultual assistance in Paraguay, and various
other examples in Latin America. The idea of credit financing is well
established and acceptable in Latin America, but more unfamiliar in many
other developing countries.

Dominguez (1973) for example, suggests that "cultural values and
attitudes determine the use of credit", and cites the examples of France
and the USA, where total bank debts amounted to 28 and 88 per cent of GNP
respectively, in 1969. He gives figures for five Latin American countries
ranging from 16 per cent of GNP in Jamaica to 41 per cent in Colombia.
However, when he then uses these figures to draw conclusions about the
economic feasibility of loan programs, and to determine the maximum size
of a student loan fund he encounters problems. He suggests that "Logical
reasoning would lead us to predict that the maximum amount of capital" for
a student loan institution in Jamaica would be 0.64 of GNP, whereas in
fact the Students' Loan Bureau of Jamaica had capital amounting to 1.16
per cent of GNP in 1971, which is almost double the figure he predicted,
and beyond the threshold of feasibility according to his argument. He
concludes "Although the total amount of credit existing in a country might
be a useful indicator, it is susceptible to political manipulations as
well as to technological innovation. Credit cards are an example of such
an innovation. Student Loan institutions may well be another" (Dominguez
1973, p. 113)

Dominguez devotes considerable attention to the question of the
threshold of economic feasibility of student loan programs and how to
establish capital ceilings and debt ceilings for students. He suggests
that 3 per cent of GNP is probably the limit of economic feasibility for a
student loan program and shows that because of the very high level of
students' living expenses in many developing countries a student loan

program would have to exceed this in order to have a significant social impact. His comparision of students' living expenses in relation to per capita national income in developing countries and developed countries (shown in Table 5.1) is very revealing, showing as it does that in about 1970 student living expenses in developing countries averaged two or three times the level of per capita national income, compared with only half in France or the USA.

This helps to explain why, for example Brodersohn (in IDB 1978) concludes that it would not be practicable for loan schemes to cover both tuition fees and living expenses, because it would impose too great a burden of debt, and also why he argues that loans can be used to finance secondary or higher educaton, but not both. It also explains why loan programs in Latin America have often had to reply on external funding, because of the magnitude of the capital required. Certainly experience in many developing countries supports the conclusion of Dominguez and Sirken (World Bank Case Study and Exercise Series 1980) that "A revolving fund to continuously finance a cohort of students requires an enormous committment of capital. Because the amount required to initiate a student loan institution is normally small in comparision with total needs, people and governments have frequently underestimated the capital required". This does not mean that a student loan insitution is not feasible, because of its capital requirements, but simply that it must be realistically costed, and not expected to become self financing quickly.

On the question of political feasibility, experience is conflicting. Rogers, Fields and Williams for example all conclude that loan schemes are politically feasible in Africa, even if they are likely to be initially unpopular. Yet the experience of Ghana and Nigeria suggests that governments are unwilling to alienate students by introducing loans and increasing fees. Perhaps the experience of Norway provides a clue to a solution. When the student loan scheme was first introduced graduates could claim tax relief on loan repayments (as they still can in the USA). However this tax concession was later withdrawn and the government revenue saved by the change was allocated to scholarships for secondary school pupils. By linking the two measures, and giving publicity to the need to finance the new scholarships, the government was able to overcome resistance to the change. Certainly Williams suggests that in Ghana massive publicity was needed to convince the public of the need for loans in higher education, and he explains the unpopularity of the loan scheme partly in terms of the failure to attempt such a publicity campaign. Similarly, Rogers concludes: "There is no question, but that the institution of tuition fees where none existed before is a politically unpopular action. On the other hand, a sensible propoganda campaign pointing out the distributional effects of such an action should be able to generate widespread support" (Rogers 1970).

The argument that loans are not administratively feasible in developing countries is also not supported by the facts, even though there have undoubtedly been problems with collection and default rates in many countries. However, experience suggests these problems can be reduced, if not totally solved.

TABLE 5.1

STUDENTS' LIVING EXPENSES AND PER CAPITA GNP

	Country	Year	St.Expenses	GNP	(4)
LDC's	Brazil	1972	5,650 Crs	2,094 Crs	2.70 GNP
	Chile [1]	1970	40,000 E [1]	6,282 E	6.36 GNP
	Dom.Republic	1970	$1,000	$311	3.22 GNP
	Ghana	1972	650 NC	248 NC	2.62 GNP
	Mexico	1970	$17,200	$7,743	2.22 GNP
HDC's	France	1971	8,500 Fr.	16,666 Fr.	.51 GNP
	Spain I [3]	1970	75,000 Pts [3]	69,666 Pts	1.07 GNP [3]
	II [3]	1970	65,000 Pts [3]	69,644 Pts	.93 GNP [3]
	USA	1972	$2,930	$5,119	.57 GNP
	Denmark	1967/68	7,300 Kr	18,970 Kr	.38 GNP
	Norway	"	6,544 Kr	15,907 Kr	.41 GNP
	Sweden	"	7,980 Kr	18,300 Kr	.43 GNP
	Finland	"	4,510 FMk	8,115 FMk	.56 GNP

based on the maximum annual values allowed for financial help.

(1) The value might be overstated, for it is given by a foreigner financed by an international scholarship, in dollars.

(2) Not in the capital, in Medellin. The capital would register a larger figure, probably 2.2 GNP

Source: Dominguez, 1973

LOANS AS A COST-RECOVERY MECHANISM

It has been repeatedly emphasised that loan schemes do not provide an opportunity to make higher education completely self-financing in any LDC, at least on the basis of experience so far. The conclusion of Kausel, on Latin America programs (in IDB 1978) is shared by many others:

"The effectiveness of educational credit as a significant source of financing for higher education is doubtful". This is because long repayment periods, subsidised interest rates and collection problems all reduce the potential revenue from loan repayments. Kausel therefore concludes that student loans are "not a mechanism a government adapts to gain quick political benefits: it is a decision that requires a medium-term political horizon" (Kausel 1978, p.341)

Other studies of loan schemes in Latin America come to similar conclusions. Herrick et.al. (1974) suggest that it will be 10 to 20 years before a revolving fund can approach self-financing. Brodersohn (in IDB 1978) quotes a study of student loans in El Salvador, which attempted to quantify the financing requirements of a 10 year lending program for both secondary and higher education; it showed that the capital requirement would be very substantial and even in the tenth year of the program, loan amostization would cover only 8.3 per cent of the loans granted in that year, and Brodersohn therefore emphasises "the limited possibility of a student loan program becoming a significant instrument for solving the problems of financing higher education" (Brodersohn, 1978, p. 164).

Yet though loans cannot solve the problems of financing higher education, there is evidence that they can contribute to a solution, and without a system of loans the problem may get much worse, given the very high levels of subsidy in developing countries. The fact that costs per university student are so much higher in developing countries than in developed countries points to the need for a two-pronged attack on the problem of financing. Cost reduction measures are vitally important, and will bring quicker savings. However, in a situation of long-run financial constraints medium and long run savings are worth pursuing, as well as quick savings, and loan schemes do offer significant long run savings.

There is also ample evidence that student loan schemes can successfully involve non-government capital, for example from commercial banks in Colombia, Israel, or from public and private enterprises, as in Colombia, or donations from private organisations or trade unions, such as APLUB in Brazil. If private sources are able to provide a share of the capital needed to establish a loan fund this will reduce the burden on public funds. Dominguez (1973) argues for "financially sound student loan institutions to become part of the national banking system". Many of the institutions in developing countries are too recent for this to be possible, but the experience of several Latin American countries, particularly Argentina, Colombia and Peru, and also Israel, show that the banking system can be involved in the financing of student loans, and the schemes in Sri-Lanka and Pakistan show that commercial banks, whether private or nationalized can administer, as well as finance student loans.

Daniels concludes his evaluation of Latin American institutions very positively:- "One aspect of these programs that is clearly successful is the generation of new funds for education. In the short run new funds are generated through interested aid donors and donations of private individuals, companies and foundations. These funds can be used time and again as loans to students and repaid" (Rogers, February 1972). However, he adds "The programs are not providing long run resources for education from one source that seems a natural: the substitution of loans for free education....The great impact that these programs could have would come from the substitution of loans for services (education, room, board etc) that are presently provided free or very highly subsidized....A significant new source of funds for education would be generated" (Rogers February 1972, p.27).

Similarly, Jallade concludes, on the basis of his evaluation of ICETEX in Colombia "Loans cannot be considered as a source of finance for public universities simply because those universities do not charge significant tuition fees..When the loan scheme was launched, very little, if anything, was done to alter the pattern of financing of Colombian universities with a view to increasing the role of fees... In the absence of any reform of university finance, it is hard to see how ICETEX performance could be improved in this area". (Jallade 1974, p.35)

In other words, the extent to which a loan scheme can create a new source of finance by acting as an effective cost-recovery mechanism is a policy choice, and Developing countries have chosen not to adopt this policy. The implications of this, and other policy choices, will be dicussed in Section VII.

FLEXIBILITY

Although it is a fairly recent development, many countries are now exploring the possibility of using variations in loan repayment terms as incentives, and thus making loan schemes more flexible as a financing mechanism. The recent developments in the lending policy of Educredito in Honduras, for example, which include loan forgiveness clauses for students from the most disadvantaged families, or for those who achieve very good results, or who enter shortage occupations, show that the importance of the flexibility of loans, particularly when used in association with grants, or when converted into grants for selected students, is now receiving greater emphasis in Latin America.

The fact that loan forgiveness clauses, together with interest charges, repayment periods and other conditions of loans can all be manipulated, in order to achieve particular goals of efficiency or equity means that loans are a very flexible method of subsidising students. For example, the new policy of Educredito in Honduras, which is being encouraged by IDB is to provide "loan/grants". These are explained by IDB as follows:-

> "Under the loan/grant system, a loan is made at the beginning of a course, but a portion of its repayment is waived on its successful completion, along with other requirements that the student must meet" (IDB 1981).

In other words, whether a student receives a loan or a grant will depend upon the student's performance and various criteria such as the expected income level of the occupation for which the student is trained.

Similarly, the fact that in Israel students may choose between a loan and a grant of 35 per cent of the value of the loan is another example of the potential flexibility of loan/grant mechanisms.

One of the most flexible kinds of student loan - the income contingent loan - has not yet been introduced in any developing countries, although several schemes do have variable repayment schemes to allow for different levels of income. Colombia, however, does have a system of fees which vary with students income and for the future, the possibility of variable terms loans combined with variable fees may offer considerable scope for flexibility in financing higher education.

EFFICIENCY

Advocates of loans in developing countries suggest various ways in which they could contribute to efficiency. By reducing the level of subsidy and so bringing the private and social rate of return closer together, loans can lead to a more efficient use of resources, since a massive subsidy, such as exists in many developing countries may lead to over-investment by individuals in higher education. Loans may also contribute to greater efficiency within institutions, by improving the motivation, and performance of students and making them more cost-conscious.

Herrick et.al. conclude from their examination of Latin American experience that loans can contribute the increases in efficiency:

"There is good evidence that students receiving education credit will be more apt to complete their education, and to do so in less time than those who do not receive credit. The credit enables the student borrower to continue his education in the first instance, or to devote more time to it if he has had to be self-supporting. His assumption of an obligation to pay for the education gives him the motivation to qualify himself for better paying employment and to complete his course of study as quickly as possible, thus keeping his total obligation to a minimum"

(Herrick et al. 1974, p.20)

Their study quotes three examples:

1) IFARHU of Panama found that 90 per cent of all students financed under its program complete their studies successfully, a far higher percentage than among students as a whole.

2) INCE of Argentina, where students are not eligible for loans until after they have successfully completed part of their course, found that students finished their course at least a year earlier than those without loans.

3) A study in Colombia showed that the academic achievement of students with credit is better than that of the average

student. Attribution of cause and effect, however, is difficult, because the student who receives credit may be the more highly motivated student in the first instance.

In fact, Jallade's study of Colombia suggests that because loans are awarded by ICETEX selectively, borrowers will differ from non-borrowers in terms of ability and motivation. He found that repeat rates were low among ICETEX borrowers but again, concludes that this does not prove that loans reduce wastage. The lower wastage may be because loans act as incentives to students to work harder or may simply reflect their above average ability (Jallade 1974, p.31).

It is therefore difficult to find any conclusive evidence on the effects of loans on internal efficiency, but the fact that developments such as the "loan/grant" in Honduras specifically link loan forgiveness clauses with student performance show that loan institutions in Latin America are trying to use loans as an incentive to greater efficiency.

EQUITY

The question of the effect of student loans on equality of opportunity and on equity raises two issues:-

1) whether loans increase the educational opportunities of poor students;

2) whether loans redistribute the costs of higher education, to bring about a more equitable distribution of costs and benefits.

This is an area where advocates of loans make the most optimistic claims, since it is well known that there are enormous inequalities of access in developing countries and that existing methods of finance favour the rich, who benefit most from higher education, at the expense of lower income taxpayers who help to subsidise them.

Because of the high hopes of the advocates of loans, the actual performance of loan programs in developing countries seems, at first, disappointing. There is no doubt that loans are awarded to students from low income families but the overall impact on equality of opportunity has proved less than was hoped, and it is still true that higher income families receive much greater educational subsidies than poor families.

Herrick et al. (1974) provide a number of examples of how loan programs have benefitted low-income students in Latin America, but conclude that the contribution of loans to increasing opportunities for poor students has been limited because:

a) programs are concentrated at post-secondary level, where only about 1 per cent of the eligible population enrols. Genuine equality of opportunity demands much greater assistance at the secondary level, where poor pupils drop out for financial reasons;

b) the desire to produce quick results, from the point of

view of adding to trained manpower leads to a concentration on high ability students, or students who are already enrolled, and will complete their course quickly.

c) the desire to develop a sound financial base for a revolving fund leads to a concentration on students who are a "good risk".

d) the requirement that students provide personal guarantees or collateral discriminates against the poor.

Finally, the study concludes that "only the poorest of the applicants (most of whom are at least lower middle class) can be reached - not the poorest of the people". (Herrick et al. 1974, p.4)

Similarly, Jallade (1974) concludes that "the student loan scheme run by ICETEX shows a rather limited ability to bring educational opportunities to those who lack them" (Jallade 1974, p.36).

Like the earlier study, Jallade's evaluation stresses that equity and manpower goals frequently conflict, and in such cases, most programs give preference to the manpower goals. He also stresses that "student loans may contribute to "democratize" higher education only if secondary education has been "demoncratized" before. (Jallade 1974, p.40)

His final conclusions on the equity implications of student loans in Colombia are that:

1) In spite of ICETEX intentions, the population of loan receipients remains strongly biased in favour of the priveleged groups when compared to Colombian society;

2) ICETEX loans contribute much more to the financing of private universities than to the financing of public ones, (See Table 5.2) and private sector recipients have much higher family incomes than students at public universities (See Table. 5.3).

3) The ICETEX loan scheme "can hardly be considered as a tool to shift the burden of higher education away from taxpayers to students, but rather, as a cheaper way to channel additional funds to private universities and public sector students than would be the case with outright grants". (Jallade 1974, p.35)

This rather pessimistic conclusion on the equity effects of student loans has tended to reduce confidence in loans as a mechanism for financing education. If they do not have much impact in redistributing opportunities or financial burdens why should developing countries go to the expense and trouble to introduce loan schemes?

The answer is partly that loans must be compared with other methods of subsidising education, and as Rogers emphasises "student loan programs probably lead to less inequity than that which would prevail

TABLE 5.2

STUDENT LOANS AND THE FINANCING OF UNIVERSITIES IN COLOMBIA

	1969 Public Universities	1969 Private Universities	1970 Public Universities	1970 Private Universities
1. Total university revenue(a) (Thousand Pesos)	707,300	210,100	776,600	269,400
2. Total revenue originating from tuition fees(a) (Thousand Pesos)	39,150	146,000	37,800	187,000
3. Tuition fees as a proportion of total revenue (2/1 x 100)	5.5	69.5	4.9	69.4
4. Number of ICETEX loans(b)	5,720	3,480	6,640	3,560
5. Average amount of loan (Pesos)	4,360	6,320	4,470	6,230
6. Average amount of tuition finance per loan (Pesos)	260	4,430	290	4,520
7. Total tuition fees financed through ICETEX loans (6 x 4 thousand Pesos)	1,490	15,420	1,930	16,090
8. Loan-financed tuition fees as a proportion of total revenue from tuition fees (7/2 x 100)	3.8	10.6	5.1	8.6
9. Loan-financed tuition fees as a proportion of total university revenue (7/1 x 100)	0.2	7.3	0.2	6.0

Source: Jallade 1974, Table 9

TABLE 5.3

VOLUME OF LOANS ACCORDING TO FAMILY INCOME OF THE RECIPIENTS OVER THE

1969 - 71 PERIOD, COLOMBIA

Income Brackets (Pesos/year)	Family Size	Family Income (%)	Number of of Loans (%)	Average Amount of Loan (Pesos)	Total Amount Borrowed (%)
Public Universities					
0 - 18000	5.4	8.1	37.7	4440	36.6
18000 - 36000	5.7	17.4	26.2	4460	25.7
36000 - 54000	6.0	17.0	15.0	4730	15.1
54000 - 72000	5.6	11.7	7.4	5100	8.3
72000 -120000	5.5	19.2	8.4	4260	7.9
Over 120000	5.5	26.6	5.3	5460	6.5
Total	5.6	100.0	100.0	4580	100.0
Private Universites					
0 - 18000	5.1	2.3	18.3	5890	16.5
18000 - 36000	5.3	7.6	20.8	5970	19.1
36000 - 54000	5.2	9.5	16.3	6100	14.5
54000 - 72000	5.0	8.5	9.9	6800	10.4
72000 -120000	4.5	22.2	17.6	7200	19.3
Over 120000	5.0	49.9	17.1	7700	20.2
Total	5.0	100.0	100.0	6570	100.0

Figures may not add due to rounding.

Source: Jallade 1974 - Table 18

without them" (Rogers February 1972, p.16). The other answer which is stressed by all the relevant studies, is that loan programs must be accompanied by changes in fee policy, and an increase in aid at the secondary level, if the full impact of loans is to be achieved. Once again, this emphasises that the introduction of loans alone is not enough, but should be accompanied by fundamental changes in fee levels.

MANPOWER

Several of the studies have already emphasised that where manpower and equity goals conflict, preference is usually given to manpower. Many of the programs give preference to subjects or occupations considered to be in short supply, and adding to the stock of trained manpower is a major goal of all programs. Rogers concludes, of the Latin American programs that "increasing the output of high level manpower in developmental fields, the main explicit objective... is being successfully met to a great degree" (Rogers, February 1972, p.26).

Herrick et.al. conclude that all programs are making a general impact on manpower development, but argue that this impact could be increased by greater use of variations in loan repayment terms and other incentives as a manpower tool and greater concentration on research: "A student loan program is most effective if the institution combines its responsibility for financial administration with continuing programs of research into Manpower needs, evaluation of the impact of the program on individual and social needs, and development of testing and counseling services" (Herrick et al. 1974, p.3).

On the question of incentives, the study notes that no country yet makes systematic use of loan forgiveness as an instrument of manpower policy. Since this was written the practice has begun to grow, for example in Colombia, and Honduras. A note of warning is sounded however:

> "Forgiveness policies may be effective and useful to a limited degree.. (but) the forgiveness factor does not keep all students for more than a year or so in the fields they originally choose. According to a recent study in Jamaica, the majority of loan recipients did not continue to work in the specific field in which they had been trained". (Herrick et al. 1974, p.14).

Similarly, Jallade (1974) concludes that ICETEX has contributed both to the supply of educated manpower and to its structure, but ICETEX lending policies could be even more selective by increasing the "incentive power" of loans, for example by providing different levels of subsidy for different subjects or fields of study.

Finally, on the subject of brain drain, the evidence is reassuring. Rogers quotes evidence from Colombia that "brain drain fears appear unwarranted, since only 2.3 per cent of the students who studied abroad with ICETEX assistance have remained abroad... the fear of emigration, from Colombia at least, seems to have been grossly exaggerated". (Rogers, February 1972, p.11).

ADMINISTRATION

Reference has already been made to the two most frequent problem, late repayments and defaults, and to attempts to reduce these. Rogers concludes, on the basis of the limited evidence available in 1972, that "the rate of default in the long run will be low".

Herrick et.al. conclude that "the experience of collection problems, in the United States as well as in Latin America, suggests that the most effective collection agents must be used - and in many countries these would be the banks". They cite the example of Brazil, where banks have been successful in reducing the costs of collection (Herrick et.al 1974. p.35). However the experience of the People's Bank in Sri Lanka shows that banks also have a poor record of collection in some developing countries.

The experience in Sri Lanka also suggests that it may be important to lengthen the "grace period", since many graduates take more than two years to find work. This underlines the importance of seperating those who wish to postpone repayment of their loan, due to unemployment, from genuine defaulters. If borrowers have the opportunity to renegotiate repayment terms in cases of difficulty, the problem of default is much reduced.

The general conclusion seems to be that the formidable administrative problems of establishing student loan funds in developing countries can be overcome, particularly where there is a well established banking sector, but a successful loan institution needs high quality management, assisted by the latest techniques of data processing. Sharing of experience, for example through APICE in Latin America, also seems to be an important way in which the administration of student loans can be improved and both AID and IBD have provided technical assistance to improve the administration of loan programs in Latin America. This is one example of the contribution of international aid, and the following section looks at this in greater detail.

SECTION VI

THE ROLE OF INTERNATIONAL AGENCIES

Both IDB and US AID have been important in providing financial and technical assistance in establishing student loan programs in Latin America. Both are still actively engaged in providing such assistance, although there has been a reduction in the involvement of AID in financing student loans in recent years dueto a shift in the priorities of its lending policies. The World Bank has financed research on student loans in Colombia, but has not financed student loan programs.

US AGENCY FOR INTERNATIONAL DEVELOPMENT

During the 1960's and early 1970's AID gave financial or technical assistance to student loan institutions in six Latin American countries: Colombia, Dominican Republic, Ecuador, Honduras, Nicaragua, and Peru, and a student loan program in Brazil had benefitted from a counterpart loan generated by AID program loans. It was on the basis of this experience that Herrick e. al. carried out their evaluation of education credit institutions in Latin America, looking specifically at the implications for AID. More recently AID has provided assistance for Costa Rica and Panama, and provided a further loan for the Dominican Republic.

Table 6.1 shows the grants or loans that had been provided by AID at the time of Herrick's study in 1974. This shows that the largest loans went to ICETEX in Colombia, FCE in the Dominican Republic and Educredito in Honduras. PEBE in Brazil received the largest amount, though this was in the form of counterpart loans.

On the subject of disbursement of AID loans, Herrick reports "no major problems" in Colombia, where portions of Education Sector Loans III, IV, and V were allocated for ICETEX programs, in the Dominican Republic, where two AID loans had moved as planned, and in Honduras, where an AID loan was disbursed faster than planned because Ecucredito raised the required share of its own funds faster than anticipated.

The study draws the following conclusions and implications from the Latin American experience for AID:

> "(1) In terms of timely disbursement of AID loans, the support of education credit institutions has not posed problems.However, success in providing sufficient seed capital to put the institution on a sound financial basis for a continuing program has not been achieved. Furthermore, the initial support from AID will not, in all instances, have been sufficient, in combination with the efforts of the institution itself, to achieve the leverage required to obtain additional financing from other sources.
>
> (2) AID must recognize that under present conditions a credit institution will require capital infusions for more than 10 years to maintain a given program level and longer to support an expanding program. Changes in conditions (such as higher interest

TABLE 6.1

LOANS AND GRANTS FROM US. AID

FOR EDUCATIONAL CREDIT INSTITUTIONS UP TO 1974

Country	Institution Acronym	Full Name	AID Grants ($ Millions)	AID Loans ($ Millions)
Brazil	PEBE	Programa Especial de Bolsas de Estudo	–	(11.9)[a]
Colombia	ICETEX	Instituto Colombiano de Credito Educativo y Estudios Tecnicos en el Exterior	0.2	4.7
Ecuador	IECE	Instituto Ecuatoriano de Credito Educativo	<0.1	–
Dominican Republic	FCE	Fundacion de Credito Educativo	0.5[b]	3.2
Honduras	Educredito		<0.1	2.0
Nicaragua	INDE	Instituto Nicaraguense de Desarrollo: Educredito	0.3	–
Peru	IPFE	Instituto Peruano de Fomento Educativo	0.4	–

Source: Herrick et.al. 1974

Notes : a from counterpart generated by AID program loans
        b plus government grants from funds generated by AID

The study by Herrick et al. quotes the following AID reports:

US Department of State. Agency for International Development Capital Assistance Paper. "Chile: Human Resources Development Loan". AID-DLC/P-835. June 24, 1969

- "Colombia-Education Sector Loan V". AID-DLC/P-1095
- "Colombia-Education Sector Loan III". AID-DLC-/P-965 May 28, 1971.
- "Colombia-Education Section LOan IV". AID-DLC/P-1019. May, 11, 1972.
- "Dominican Republic: Educational Credit" AID-DLC/P-585 June 1, 1967
- "Dominican Republic- Educational Credit" AID-DLC/P-895 May, 7 1970
- "Ecuador: Educational Credit". AID-DLC/P-990. September 23, 1971.
- "Honduras -Student Loan Fund - Educredito". AID-DLC/P-963
- "Nicaragua: Education Sector Loan". AID-DLC/P-1035

rates and shorter amortization periods for student loans) might alleviate the cash flow deficits in the earlier years of a program, but these probably would not be totally sufficient."

(3) "In order to obtain a faster return on student loans, and thus shorten the loan-repayment cycle turnover, AID might encourage application of the following measures:

- higher interest rates, close to or at commercial rates.
- shorter grace periods
- shorter amortization periods
- limitations on period of study financed
- maintenance of value provisions
- enforceable guaranties
- sizeable delinquency penalties
- effective tools of collection (salary garnishes, etc)

However, there may be practical or policy consideration militating against applying all these methods; for example, debt burden may become too high in relation to the earning power of the student graduate, or policy may favor the financing of a full university course of 4 to 6 years instead of the last years only. But there is little excuse for not making provision for maintenance of value and not systematically invoking penalties and enforcing collection (as some institutions have done in the past".

(4) "Education loan programs are reaching individual post-secondary students with academic ability and relatively great economic need. But so far, with the exception of a secondary level scholarship program in Colombia and a special program for dependents of union members in Brazil, they have had little impact in broadening opportunities for the majority of the young population that will never finish secondary school. If AID programs are to be designed to focus on low-income groups in the population, assistance to education at higher levels, even if it emphasizes programs to reach disadvantaged students, will not do the trick. In order to reach young people who have not already been selected out of the system by economic and social factors, the problems must be attacked at the secondary and primary levels".

(5) "Education credit institutions face a number of administrative problems. They tend to grow fast, outgrowing internal control mechanisms, and they frequently underestimate the organization and management capability they will need. In contemplating assistance to any such institution, especially one that has been established relatively recently, or one that is now planning expansion of its program, AID should expect to have to work closely with its management on a continuing basis".

(6) "Credit institutions should have as broad a mandate as possible in the substance of their business. In other words, they are most effective if they not only administer a wide range of programs (for loans and scholarships) but also are involved in

manpower planning, vocational and academic guidance, research on
the impact of manpower training, job placement, and creation of
imaginative proposals for further expanding educational
opportunities and financing. They may use banking resources to
finance or subsidize their programs, but they are not banks nor
should they try to be. AID should encourage them to delegate loan
disbursement and collection and possibly other administrative
tasks, to other organizations as much as possible in order to
reduce overhead and to lessen distractions from the principal
functions of the institution. Furthermore, banks may well have
greater success in handling the loans on a business-like basis"

(Herrick et al. 1974, p.7-8)

Since the mid 1970's AID has been less involved in financing
student loan institutions, but this does not appear to be due to doubts
about their effectiveness, since no further evaluations have been carried
out since Herrick's, but because of changing priorities within lending
programs, and an increased emphasis on projects which will help the
poorest sections of the community, and less emphasis on higher education.

However, in 1981 a further loan was given to the Dominican
Republic to finance student loans given by FCE for vocational education.
The project report states "FCE has acquired a unique kind of flexibility
not found elsewhere:

1) FCE provides educational credits to a wide variety of
categories - at the professional, administrative and
technical levels.

2) FCE's loan recipients may study in-country or abroad, and
pursue degree or non-degree programs.

3) FCE's board of directors includes public and private
decision makers in the country;

4) FCE provides institutional loans for initiating or raising
the quality of educational programs

5) The Foundation has valuable experience and a capability to
deal with problems in the supply of human resources at the
vocational, technical, managerial and professional levels"

(AID, 1981, p.4)

The purpose of the loan is to provide capital to finance loans to
between 3,000 and 4,000 students taking vocational courses and loans to
vocational school teachers to allow them to upgrade their own
qualifications. FCE has already received two AID loans, the first ($1.4
million) helped to establish the Foundation, and a second ($1.7million)
was designed to strengthen its lending capacity. The fact that AID is
providing a third loan is therefore evidence of its confidence in the
institution, and on the basis of analysis of its operations and actual and
projected cash flow the project concludes:-

1) "it is considered a responsible and adequate student credit institution

2) The efforts made by the management in enforcing collections on delinquent loans and increasing new loan portfolios are very effective, which serve to demonstrate its ability to cover its costs.

3) "the organization and institutional capacity of FCE appears to be adequate and efficient in the administration of educational portfolio without major increments in the operating cost. FCE projects that its total receipts will double from $2.4 million in 1981 to $4.9 million in 1989. Major growth is expected to be in recoveries of loans granted from its own portfolio" AID 1981, pp. 54-5.

The report does identify certain administrative weaknesses, for example "excesive paperwork in loan collection but in general, the administration of FCE seems sound.

The project reports includes not only analysis of FCE's past lending, but also analysis of the proposed expansion, including a discussion of the cash-flow of borrowers, which concludes "there appears to be no question of the students' ability to meet repayment obligations out of their anticipated future earnings under the planned loan terms". Finally it discusses FCE's own cash flow and concludes:

1) "It is interesting to note that by 1988 credit approval of $3.0 million could be supported by an FCE contribution of $2.0 million and a rollover fund of around $1 million. Interest income plus private contributions should be sufficient to cover operating costs and unless a significant increase in demand takes place by 1988, FCE should be able to operate without additional government support or foreign loans.

2) Financial projections indicate that a viable revolving fund devise will emerge despite restrictive assumptions such as 10 per cent interest rate, a 25 per cent delinquency rate, a 7 per cent default rate and an increasing inflationary rate" (AID 1981, pp 73-74).

This project report is of considerable interest in showing the careful analysis and planning that must precede the introduction of a new loan program, and in showing that student loans for vocational education seem perfectly feasible in the Dominican Republic. The AID loan is an example of how new credit for vocational education can be created with the help of a foreign aid agency, and this report shows how careful analysis of the operation of a student loan institution can help to improve its efficiency.

INTER-AMERICAN DEVELOPMENT BANK

Six countries in Latin America and the Caribbean have received loans from IDB financed from its Fund for Special Operations to enable them to establish or expand educational credit institutions. Table 6.2 shows the countries and institutions which have received loans from IDB. In the case of Panama, Jamaica and Honduras IDB has made second loans, so that once again this reflects the continued confidence of an international aid agency in the operations of student loan institutions.

The first loan given by IDB to a student loan institution was given, in 1966, to Panama, and marked an innovation in IDB lending, since previously the Bank had made loans only to universities or other advanced education institutions to enable them to finance capital projects. The press release announcing this new type of loan stressed the manpower implications, and stated that "the program is in line with Panama's National and Economic Development Plan.. in which a high priority is assigned to increasing the number of university, vocational and technical graduates, as a means of speeding up the achievement of the Plan's goals" (IDB 88/SF PN)

However, by the time IDB announced a loan to Trinidad and Tobago in 1972 it also emphasised that the loans would go to help students from low or medium-income families. The manpower goal was still emphasised, but the goal of expanding opportunities was also emphasised and the announcement also added "It will create a permanent mechanism to assure continued support for higher education in selective fields" (IDB 336/SF/TT)

The first loan to Jamaica was made in 1970, and by 1976 IDB made a new loan, to allow the Students' Revolving Fund to expand, and the announcement stated "Since its establishment in 1970, this credit program has constituted an integral part of the Jamaican educational system and has benefitted a wide segment of the country's student population. By providing repayable resources to expand financial accessibility to higher and vocational education opportunities, the Government of Jamaica will allocate its limited educational resources in a more rational and effective manner and will help relieve inflationary pressures on the cost of education and on the cost of living in general" (IDB 466/SF JA)

The loan to Honduras, granted for Educredito, in 1976, included $42,000 in technical co-operation to finance the hiring of consultants to advise Educredito on administrative procedures, and the loan announcement explained that "owing to financial limitations, Educredito - which was established in 1968 - has not been able to meet the rising demand for student loans. In the 8-year period from 1968 to 1975 the agency granted 1,741 loans to students in the amount of $4,406,000. In 1975 it granted 358 loans which represented 35 per cent of the students who formally contacted the program" (IDB 489/SF/HO). This loan was intended to provide extra credit, therefore, to enable Educredito to expand, and by 1981, when a second IDB loan was granted, the announcement referred to the earlier project and said "The goal of that project was the training of 515 students. The goal was substantially exceeded and some 866 undergraduate and graduate students in various disciplines benefitted. (IDB 657/SF-HO).

TABLE 6.2

LOANS FROM IDB FOR EDUCATIONAL CREDIT INSTITUTIONS

1966 - 81

Loan No	Country	Institution Acronym	Institution Full Name	Year	IDB Loan ($ Million)
88/SF-PN	Panama	IFARHU	Instituto para la Formacion y Aprovechamiento de Recursos Humanos	1966	0.7
283/SF-JA	Jamaica	SLB	Students Loan Bureau	1970	4.7
292/SF-PN	Panama	IFARHU		1971	1.4
336/SF-TT	Trinidad & Tobago	SRLF	Students Revolving Loan Fund	1972	3.7
466/SF-JA	Jamaica	SLB		1976	5.9
489/SF-HO	Honduras	EDUCREDITO	Instituto de Credito Educativo	1976	3.0
500/SF-CR	Costa Rica	CONAPE	Comision Nacional de Prestamos para Educacion	1977	4.8
503/SF-BA	Barbados	SRLF	Students Revolving Loan Fund	1977	0.8
657/SF-HO	Honduras	EDUCREDITO		1981	7.5

Source: IDB

Thus the continued involvement of IDB in financing educational credit in Latin America is evidence of its continued confidence in the concept of student loans. This does not mean that there have been no problems. IDB has carried out a number of technical assessments and analysis of student loan institutions, and these have been summarised by Ibacache (1978) His report identifies certain problems, for example a high level of defaults in Jamaica, but he concludes that the technical, socio-economic, financial and political complexities of educational credit have been clarified by the analysis carried out by the Bank, and by the accumulation of experience, although several of the programs are too recent to allow full evaluation.

Since this was written IDB has continued to carry out analysis of individual programs and to suggest improvements. For example the new loan to Honduras involves the creation of "loan/grants" which will provide incentives for performance and will provide loan forgiveness clauses for selected students. This is an example of how IDB is seeking to develop the concept of educational credit, by making it available for new types of education, including technical and vocational as well as university education, and by making student loans more flexible as a financing mechanism.

The analysis of student loan institutions by IDB includes the construction of a computer model which can be used to determine capital requirements and cash flow of a loan program. This is another example of how international agencies can improve the efficiency of student loan institutions as well as contribute to their financing.

THE WORLD BANK

The World Bank has not provided financial aid to student loan institutions. However, the Bank did finance research into the operations of ICETEX (Jallade 1974) which drew the following conclusions from the Colombian experience for other developing countries which are considering whether or not to embark on student loans: "At least three conditions must be met if this question is to be answered positively:

1) The first condition is to consider student loans for what they actually are, i.e. a policy tool to achieve such educational objectives as altering (i) the size and structure of the supply of educated manpower, (ii) the social composition of the student body, and (iii) the amount and the origin of funds devoted to education. If any of these alterations are actually needed in a given country, then loans can be envisaged.

    The rich experience of Colombia shows that there is no rigid, universal relationship between the objectives sought for and student loans per se. Whether a set of objectives will be achieved or not depends entirely on the particular characteristics of the loan scheme under consideration. To put it otherwise, there are nearly as many types of student loans as objectives considered.

    In the field of education, policy-makers and planners are

often pursuing different, <u>conflicting</u>, goals at the same time. The temptation to use a new policy tool such as student loans to achieve everything at the same time is always present.

2) It is necessary to assess the existing situation in terms of educational opportunities, financial arrangements to meet the cost of education, relationship between the supply of manpower and the labor market. In this respect, the Colombian experience gives a number of useful clues. It shows, for instance, that the ability of student loans to become a non-negligible source of university revenue depends on the structure of university finance and, more specifically, on the importance of fees in total revenue. What is - and should be - the importance of fees? An agreement on this question, clearly, commands future success or failure of the scheme.

   The performance of a loan scheme vis-a-vis the equity issue is largely conditioned by the degree of equality of educational opportunity achieved in the level of education preceding the level financed by the scheme. to put it bluntly, student loans may contribute to "democratize" higher education only if secondary education has been "democratized" before.

3) Finally, it is necessary to weigh the ability of a loan system versus other student aid policies to achieve the expected objectives. As identical objectives maybe fulfilled by different student aid policies, the problem of selecting the most cost-effective one boils down to a discussion of their respective ability to achieve these objectives. Such a discussion can only take place in reference to a particular situation at a particular point in time".

(Jallade 1974, pp.38-41)

Since this project was completed a number of World Bank and other international aid agency reports on individual countries have recommended student loans as a means of changing the pattern of finance. The remainder of this paper will therefore look at the arguments for student loans in developing countries compared with other policy tools, (Section VIII) and with the policy choices to be made before a system of student loans can be introduced (Section VIII). Finally, Section IX suggests some criteria for identifying countries where further research or experimentation might take place.

SECTION VII

THE CHOICE BETWEEN STUDENT LOANS AND OTHER METHODS

OF FINANCING HIGHER EDUCATION

This paper does not attempt a review of alternative methods of financing education. Several authors have provided such a comprehensive review, for example Rogers (1970) Jallade (1973) and Zymelman (1973) and more recently Bowman (1982), Bowman, Millot and Schiefelbein (1982) and McMahon and Geske (1982). Much of this literature is concerned with general principles, or with applications of these principles in developed countries, and not all is relevant to developing countries, although there are some discussions of the particular problems of educational finance in certain regions, for example IDB (1978) on Latin America and Eicher (1982) on sub- Saharan Africa.

In this literature there is some discussion of student loans in relation to various objectives of educational finance, notably

- a) generation of adequate funds
- b) cost recovery and the redistribution of financial burdens between government and individuals
- c) efficiency
- d) equity, and the redistribution of educational opportunities
- e) optimum supply of educated manpower

There is general agreement that student loans represent a powerful tool for achieving certain objectives, for example, redistributing costs between government and individuals, but also that they are not the only possible way of achieving these objectives, and that their effectiveness will depend on what type of loan scheme is adopted, and whether loans are combined with other financing mechanisms, for example fees and scholarships.

Student loans are one way in which governments give financial assistance to students, but as earlier sections show, in almost all countries they are combined with other forms of aid:

- a) direct subsidies to institutions to enable them to provide free tuition, or to charge fees that cover only a proportion of total costs

- b) grants or scholarships awarded to students, either on grounds of academic ability or financial need, to cover all or part of fees and/or living expenses

- c) provision of free or subsidised services, including food, accommodation or travel

- d) free or subsidised books

- e) tax concessions to students or their families

f)   subsidised work-study opportunities.

Governments must choose between alternative combinations of aid to students and/or institutions.

The argument for giving finance directly to institutions, rather than students, is that this enables the government to exercise greater control over both the quantity and quality of education, and it reduces the dangers of personal patronage or favouritsm. However, many people argue that it is more efficient to provide subsidies to individuals, either through grants or through the relatively untried mechanism of vouchers, because this will increase competition between institutions, increase cost-consciousness and permit flexibility, for example the value of grants, scholarships or vouchers can be raised according to income level or rural/urban location, or subject or field of study, while fees can also vary in similar ways.

In developing countries governments provide subsidies both to institutions and individuals, but there is increasing pressure on governments to reconsider the question of fees, particularly in higher education, on grounds that this would free resources for other levels of education, would be more equitable, in view of the high private rate of return to education (Psacharopoulos 1981) and would also increase cost-consciousness. For example the IDB seminar on financing education in Latin America (IDB 1978) attempted to calculate what would be the financial impact if the higher-income groups in Latin America were to pay the total cost of their education, instead of receiving free tuition, and the public funds released in this way were used exclusively to subsidize the educatition of lower income families. The conclusion was that "The fiscal resources released by the adoption of such a measure would equal 14% of the present overall public expenditure on education". (IDB 1978, p.6). Such a policy can, therefore, be considered both on grounds of reducing the burden on public funds and on equity. It was also suggested in this seminar that "the fact is, generally speaking, that there is no cost consciousness, except in those institutions that are mainly financed by fees". (Kausel in IDB 1978, p.331).

Arguments for fees in developing countries have recently been examined by Thobani (1982) and Birdsall (1982), who suggest that it may be possible to increase efficiency in education by introducing or raising fees, without sacrificing equity. The importance of this, for the debate on student loans is that it has been demonstrated, time again, for example by Rogers (February 1971 and February 1972) and by Jallade (1974) that the effectiveness of loans as a cost recovery mechanism, as a way of redistributing financial burdens and as a way of changing the pattern of demand for education will be greatly increased if loans are accompanied by fees. If loans are introduced without changing the level of fees, then as Jallade showed in Colombia, the contribution of loans to the financing of higher education will be small (see Table 5.2) and they will do little to redistribute the costs of education between high-income students and low-income taxpayers.

Any decision about the desirability of student loans must, therefore be judged in relation to policy on fees. It must also be judged in terms of the level of subsidy to be given to individual students. As this paper shows, loans in the USA and in developing countries usually involve a "hidden grant" of up to 50 per cent of the value of the loan, because of interest subsidies. It is therefore sometimes argued that it would be better to provide all loan recipients with a grant of 25 or 35 per cent of the average value of a student loan, instead of giving them a loan or, as already happens in Israel, give students a choice between a grant or a subsidized loan. It would not cost more to give all loan recipients a smaller grant, but it might be totally ineffective, in terms of increasing opportunities for low-income students, since a grant of a quarter, or even a half of the total costs of tuition would not enable them to entrol in higher education if they were unable to raise the additional funds. This is a clear demonstration of the advantage of loans, compared with grants, namely that they enable governments to assist far more students with a given level of expenditure on student aid.

Just as loans represent only one of a range of possible methods of subsidising students, so loan repayments represent only one possible way of students discharging an obligation to society. Alternatives that have been suggested include:

1) a graduate tax, or other form of special tax for educated or professionally trained manpower

2) national service at reduced salaries for a specified period or

3) national service in specific occupations or areas.

It is often suggested that the highly educated already discharge their obligations by paying higher taxes than the less educated, or by using their skills to benefit society. For example "Graduates are in fact repaying society through their work. It is a contribution to society when doctors cure illness, engineers build roads and bridges and teachers impact knowledge and skills to their students" (Quoted in Lauglo (Ed) 1980). However, the fact that there are benefits to society (externalities) does not in itself justify the enormous subsidy most university students receive in developing countries where the cost per university student is frequently 20 or 30 times the cost per primary school pupil as in Latin America, or more than 100 times as in Ghana. The fact that graduates enjoy such high private returns, and that the private rate of return exceeds the social rate of return by a substantial margin in all developing countries is the reason why so many people argue that graduates should repay part of the costs of the education that enables them to earn high salaries. So Rogers argues against a system whereby "peasants earning a few _hundred_ dollars per year are taxed to support individuals at colleges and universities at the cost of a few _thousand_ dollars per year. (Rogers, January 1972, p. 242). He also demolishes the argument that the extra taxes already paid by graduates are sufficient repayment of the subsidy they receive : "The tax structure is aimed at having each person shoulder a portion, based on his income, of the expense of government. This is quite separate from the issue of free education or any other goverernmental service. To argue that the increase in tax yield should be considered repayment for the education is equal to arguing that individuals should be _given_ shops or other businesses by the government, as long as the taxes on their increased earnings would, on average pay back the cost of the gift". (Rogers, January 1972, p. 257).

If graduates are to repay society then, for the cost of their education, should it be by means of loan repayments, a graduate tax or national service? It was suggested in Ghana that a graduate tax would be more equitable than loans because it would affect all graduates, and not just new entrants. In Mexico, and in some other Latin American countries a special "professional tax" has been proposed. In Costa Rica an analysis of the taxes used to finance universities suggest that only 15 per cent of the total receipts comes from professionals; the remaining 85 per cent is paid by business enterprises and non-graduates (IDB 1978, p. 345). A graduate tax or "professionals' tax" would do something to remedy this.

The difference between a tax and student loans is that a graduate tax is compulsory, whereas all loan schemes are optional; it is retroactive, in the sense that it affects all graduates from the moment the tax is introduced, and it raises revenue immediately, whereas loan schemes take 10 or 20 years to generate substantial funds.

On the other hand it is argued that loans can have a positive effect on student motivation and performance, for example by encouraging them to complete their courses more quickly, and it is also suggested that a loan system would create student pressure on universities to cut costs, on the grounds that "a financing method in which the costs of education were directly visible to the financers might encourage them (i.e. the students) to press for institutional changes "leading to greater efficiency. (Rogers 1970)

The alternative to either loans or a graduate tax is a system of "bonded scholarships" or compulsory community or social service, such as exists in Tanzania and several other African countries. This has the advantage of reducing government expenditure on salaries, since most schemes involved reduced salaries for the graduates during their period of compulsory service; it may involve compulsory direction of labor, if graduates are required to work in particular areas, for example rural areas where it is hard to attract teachers or doctors. Some advocates argue that it inculcates a sense of responsibility to society, while others argue that it reduces personal freedom, which a system of loans does not.

Another way of redistributing the costs of education, particularly in the case of vocational or technical education, is a payroll tax, and these are already used in some Latin American and in some developed countries to finance vocational training. The disadvantages for developing countries, which has been emphasised by some economists in Latin America is that they may discourage employment (IDB 1978).

When all the arguments for and against loans and other methods of financing education are taken into account, it is clear that loans have certain advantages, but that whether or not they represent an optimum financing mechanism depends on the existing pattern of finance and the objectives of governments. Kausel emphasises how much those may vary, even within Latin America:

"Thus for example, Chile has been primarily endeavoring to solve an acute problem of fiscal deficit and gives overall priority to the reduction of public expenditure. In Colombia, the primary concern is with equality of opportunity, given the unequal access to education by different sectors of the population. In contrast, in Costa Rica none of the above mentioned factors is critical and consequently it is only logical to expect that there will be greater interest in university efficiency. Finally, Bolivia is at a stage where it can be assumed that considerable pressure to expand the education system, especially at the primary and secondary levels, will continue to make itself felt."

(Kausel in IDB 1978, p. 326)

Although student loans can be regarded as a "multi-purpose" tool (Jallade 1974) and as offering considerable advantages and flexibility, when compared with some other methods of finance, they should not be regarded as a panacaea, and the introduction of loans will not, by itself, solve problems of either cost recovery or equity. The experience of many developing countries, as well as developed countries, suggests that loans should be accompanied by appropriate policies on tuition fees, scholarships, or other forms of aid for very low-income students, including pupils at the secondary stage, where many of the greatest inequalities of opportunity originate, and also policies of cost-reduction and attempts to increase efficiency within institutions are needed. In other words loans should be seen as complementary rather than as an alternative to other financial measures. If loans are introduced, however, the effectiveness of the loans will depend on critical policy choices regarding the type of loans, which are examined in the next section.

SECTION VIII

POLICY CHOICES IN DESIGNING STUDENT LOAN PROGRAMS

This review of experience with student loans shows clearly that there is a wide range of types of student loan program, and any government considering the introduction of student loans faces choices concerning the objectives, the scale of the program, conditions of eligibility, the degree of subsidy and the repayment terms as well as the question of whether the program is to be administered by a specially created institution or by banks, the degree of centralisation and other administrative issues. This section considers what light can be thrown on these policy choices by experience with existing loan programs. Many of the policy choices can be seen in terms of a trade-off between different objectives, so that the final choice of conditions will be partly determined by the priority given to different goals, such as the reduction of public expenditure, equalization of opportunities, or creation of manpower.

THE TRADE OFF BETWEEN COSTS AND SELECTIVITY

The American experience with GSLP after 1978, when all students became eligible for loan subsidies presents an obvious lesson, which the Congressional Budget Office spelled out in 1981:

> "The federal role as a provider of student assistance was increased dramatically in 1978 by the passage of MISAA and the full costs of implementing it are now coming due, (when) the Congress faces increasing pressure, both internally and externally, to reduce federal spending. The trade-offs are clear. Federal benefits can continue to be distributed broadly to postsecondary students, resulting in substantially increased federal expenditures. Alternatively, funding can be reduced. Under current law, the reduction would affect lower- and moderate-income students more than others. New legislation could target federal assistance more directly on the most needy students." (Congressional Budget Office 1980, p.xi)

Some developing countries have chosen to target loan programs carefully on needy students, or give loans only for priority subject areas. The alternative, as in Ghana, is to provide loan subsidies for all students, but this greatly increases the cost to the government, and reduces the chances of the Scheme being self-financing.

If the main purpose of a loan scheme is to reduce government spending on higher education, and shift the financing burden from public to private funds, then the scheme must by highly selective, and must be linked with an increase in fees. If, on the other hand, the aim is to expand opportunities, then subsidised loans should be widely available, but this will be very costly.

One solution is to make loans widely available, but limit eligibility for interest subsidies.

THE DEGREE OF SUBSIDY OF STUDENT LOANS

Interest rates on student loans in Latin America varied in 1978 from 3 per cent to 16 per cent. The effectiveness of loans as a cost-recovery mechanism depends on the interest charged, and the length of repayment, as well as on the efficiency of collection procedures. The true cost of interest subsidies is very rarely appreciated by either the advocates or opponents of loans. Advocates of loans argue that it will be cheaper to give loans than grants; opponents argue that it will discourage students, who will be afraid to incur debts, without taking into account the substantial "hidden grant" entailed in interest rates below market rates or inflation.

A Canadian evaluation of student aid programs commented:

"Full public and student knowledge of the costs and benefits of loans is hampered by the fact that existing programs combine a guaranteed loan with non-repayable aid in the form of subsidised interest without clearly distinguishing between the two types of assistance"   (Canada: Council of Ministers, 1980, p. 113)

The lesson for any government introducing loans is clear. If these two elements are clearly distinguished, and the size of the subsidy made evident, rather than disguised, then it will help both to increase the acceptability of loans to students and the general public, and to assist realistic forecasting of future expenditure. It is partly a matter of public relations and partly a matter of planning, but in either case the subsidy needs to be clearly distinguished from the loan.

The size of the subsidy must be determined by the objectives of the program. The calculations of the revenue generated by alternative loan programs in Kenya, for example, shown in Table 4.1, shows clearly that the speed with which a fund could become self-financing depends to a considerable extent on the degree of interest subsidy. Similarly, if loans are to be written off in certain cases, if "loan/grants" are to be provided, if low-earners may automatically postpone repayment, then this will increase the degree of subsidy and reduce the revenue of the program.

Yet governments may feel that to charge realistic interest rates and shorten repayment periods would impose an intolerable burden of debt on borrowers and reduce the acceptability of loans. Much depends on how profitable higher education is for the individual, and the risks of unemployment.

EFFICIENCY AND EQUITY TRADE-OFFS

All the evaluations of loans in developing countries emphasise that governments cannot pursue manpower and equity objectives with equal fervour. Herrick suggests that where these goals conflict most Latin American loan programs favour manpower creation, but this may mean that loan subsidies will benefit high-income students more than poor.

Efficiency and equity may conflict in other ways, for example if loan institutions want to increase their self-financing capacity they will tend to concentrate funds on "good risks", who are also most likely to be high income students. If they want to use loans to reward academic achievement, or to assist high quality institutions this too may reduce their effectiveness in helping the poor.

Jallade (1974) cautions against the temptation to try to use a policy tool such as student loans "to achieve everything at the same time", and it it because some loan schemes appear to do this that they finally please nobody, since they are less effective in either generating new revenue for education or widening and redistributing opportunities, than was hoped.

As well as choosing between conflicting aims and goals, policymakers must choose which levels or types of education should be eligible for loans, and must also choose between different administrative patterns and repayment terms.

THE TRADE-OFF BETWEEN ADMINISTRATIVE COMPLEXITY AND THE COSTS OF ADMINISTRATION

Experience shows that it is possible to design very flexible loan systems, with varying levels of subsidy, such as the "loan-grant" now being developed in Honduras, with safeguards for those in low-income jobs, as in Sweden, and with different repayment terms for different occupations. It is possible to devise a very careful screening process for applicants to ensure that loans are granted to the most needy, or the most able. However every increase in the complexity of a program will increase the costs of administration. Alternatively a scheme may be very easy to administer, but will not take into account variations in personal needs, and cannot be used to create incentives, as a more flexible system could.

THE CHOICE OF ADMINISTRATIVE MODEL

There is no single administrative model for a student loan institution. The choice betwen a public and private institution; and the decision whether or not to use commercial banks, will depend very largely on political factors and banking practices. Both North and South American experience shows that commercial banks can be successfully involved in student loans; they can provide capital, and thus reduce the burden on public funds, they are often more efficient in the collection of debts than educational or other institutions. Yet experience shows that banks can sometimes be very inefficient in collecting loan repayments and do not necessarily have the expertise to make wise choices in educational, rather than commercial terms. In some countries it has been suggested that loan repayments could be collected as part of the tax collection process, but in some developing countries tax collection is known to be less efficient than the banking system. For example, the recent ILO report on Nigeria observes that tax evasion is rampant among the self employed, and concludes "It would be hard to increase the collection of direct taxes drastically in the short run. But unless tax-gathering machinery is strengthened eventually, so that all groups of society bear their proper share of taxes, inequality is likely to increase still more....A start therefore needs to be made on building up an administrative structure (which may well take ten years to complete) for efficient and objective income tax assessment and collection". (ILO 1981, p. 46). Clearly in these circumstances building up a loan collection capacity would also take a long time, and such factors have to be carefully assessed in designing a loan system.

LOAN REPAYMENT TERMS

Income-contingent loans, like a graduate tax, may involve students in a life-time committment, whereas some loan programs require borrowers to repay their debts in two or three years. The length of repayment will determine how quickly a loan fund can become self-financing. A study of El Salvador showed that if students repaid their loans over 25 years, the loan repayments would cover only a fraction of expenditure even after 10 years (IDB 1978 p. 164). However the length of repayment will also determine the burden of debt for the borrower.

Opinion is divided about whether 5 or 10 per cent of the gross income of a graduate is the maximum acceptable burden of repayment in an LDC, but very little analysis has been done of the effects of different debt burdens on students and graduates.

Obviously one very important factor is the level of unemployment among graduates. A "grace period" of six months or one year is clearly too short if, as in Sri Lanka, the majority of graduates take two years or more to find a job. Yet every increase in the "grace period" increases the costs of interest subsidies and reduces the self-financing capacity of a loan fund.

Forgiveness clauses, which are now being more widely used in developing countries have had a mixed history in developed countries, and are not regarded as a very efficient method of achieving manpower goals. For example the American experience with loan forgiveness provisions for teachers showed that such provisions were not effective as incentives (Woodhall 1970). Only time will tell how effective the concept of loan forgiveness is in Honduras for example, but it is interesting that the popularity of loan forgiveness clauses seems to be increasing in Europe as well as in developing countries.

Finally, opportunities for postponement of repayment, in cases of hardship, which are so much a feature of the Swedish loan system, would certainly increase the popularity of loans in developing countries and may be necessary at a time of growing unemployment, but this also will reduce the capacity of a loan fund to be self-financing.

THE LEVEL OF EDUCATION

Most loan schemes are intended for students in higher education; some are exclusively for university students. However, educational credit in Latin America is being extended to vocational education in several countries, for example the Dominican Republic and Honduras. In Paraguay loans are provided for vocational school graduates, to enable them to buy tools and equipment in order to put their skills into practice. Several countries now recognise the need to provide more student aid at the secondary level in order to widen access at the post-secondary level and Colombia and Brazil are both providing more scholarships for secondary school pupils, and responsibility for administering such schemes is frequently given to student loan institutions, for example ICETEX in Colombia. This raises the question of whether it is appropriate to give loans to secondary school pupils. This is done in Sweden, and it is being discussed in Latin America.

The Swedish experience suggests that if students finance both upper secondary and higher education by means of loans this creates a very large burden of debt and Brodersohn argues, on the basis of Latin American experience that "Student loans are only suitable for financing secondary or higher education, but not both (Brodershohn in IDB 1978, p.164).

On the other hand, an AID project report on the Dominican Republic concluded that "Student credit is badly needed at the secondary school technical level", and adds "Although there exist numerous problems for technical graduates at this level on the job market, and many have severe difficulties finding employment consonant with their aspirations, virtually all of them eventually find jobs in their specialties. According to staff members of these schools (as well as representatives of FCE who have given credit to students at this level) there is generally no problem in recovering loans from graduates". (AID 1981, p. 36).

Jallade concludes, from his study of student loans in Colombia:

"Although generalizing can be dangerous in such a new area of education, it seems that the future of student loans of the Colombian type is restricted to those types of education with high opportunity costs such as university or adult education. Although no experiments have ever been undertaken to finance adult education on a large scale, the characteristics of this type of education - short duration, high opportunity costs, strong expected impact on subsequent earnings, recipients' ability to provide financial guarantee - appear to be well adapted to student loan schemes".
(Jallade 1974, pp.38 - 41)

Experience suggests therefore that there may be opportunities for extending the concept of student loans beyond the field of higher education. This does not mean that it would be appropriate for one individual to finance secondary and higher and adult education by means of loans; the cumulative debt would be very large. However the Swedish system provides loans at both secondary and post-secondary levels, including loans for adults taking post-experience training but there are special provisions, which ensure that individuals who receive loans for both secondary and higher education may have part of their secondary loans written off, that is converted, retrospectively, into grants. Once again, the concept of the loan/grant, which is being introduced in Latin America, shows that loans can be an extremely flexible instrument of finance. Another possibility, which has been introduced in Ecuador, is to provide "family loans" to help parents finance secondary education for their children. (IECE 1981). The applicability of such schemes to other developing countries deserves further exploration. Certainly the lesson, from both developed and developing countries seems to be that loans need not necessarily be confined to higher education.

SECTION IX

FURTHER EXPERIMENTATION OR RESEARCH ON STUDENT LOANS

Although there is growing interest in the use of student loans in developing countries, there remain a number of doubts and uncertainties, for example on the question of debt ceilings for individuals and capital ceilings for institutions, and on the effect of alternative repayment conditions on default rates and cash flow. Several evaluations of student loan programs in Latin America were carried out in the 1970's, but although IBD and AID are both continuing to provide substantial financing assistance to loan institutions in Latin America, and though there has been evidence of changing priorities in several loan programs there has been no recent systematic evaluation of the performance of different institutions. Technical co-operation through APICE continues to be of considerable value to the institutions in Latin America, but this experience is largely unknown in other developing countries, where many of the lessons from Latin American credit institutions are extremely relevant.

The growing financial constraints upon educational expenditure in developing countries make this an appropriate time to re-open the question of using loans, in conjunction with other policies, including fees, selective scholarships and cost-reduction exercises, as a means of reducing the level of public expenditure on higher education without limiting individual opportunities.

Several recent reports by the World Bank and ILO have identified countries where student loans might be an appropriate financial mechanism. For example, the World Bank's report on the Ivory Coast states:

> "It will not be easy to find a more equitable balance between private and social benefits and costs because free public education is institutionalized and most individuals have a strong interest in retaining it. But passing on some, if not all, of the costs of education to those who benefit from it is essential if the government is to make progress in restraining future growth in enrolments, cost and unemployment among school leavers".

The recommendations of the report are that the government should consider:

> "Charging students the actual costs of education at the university and second cycle of secondary education. This action would be accompanied by a system of student loans and, in some cases where students are studying in university fields in which there are critical manpower shortages, outright grants".
> (Tuinden, den 1978, pp. 287, 297-99).

Similarly, two recent ILO reorts on Sudan and Nigeria recommend student loans. The Sudanese report suggests that "Both equity considerations and the need to transform pupils' aspirations suggest the introduction of fees (with compensatory scholarships for needy students) in secondary schools, and a student loan scheme in higher education with mandatory repayments of almost the full costs of tertiary-level schooling.

This would cut into the wholly unnecessary subsidies given to a fortunate few at present, as well as acting to reduce demand for higher education by raising the private costs of higher education up to its much greater public costs" (ILO, 1976, p. 136).

Similarly, the Nigerian report argues for a shifting of the balance between public and private finance of higher education. As Section IV showed, there is a small-scale loans scheme in Nigeria, but fees have been abolished, and the difference between private and social rates of return to higher education underlines the need for a redistribution of costs, to bring them closer into line with benefits.

There seem to be three ways in which the World Bank can contribute towards a better understanding of student loans as a financing mechanism in developing countries.

Practical research on the operations of existing student loan institutions could lead to improved understanding of the ways in which alternative types of loans affect demand for higher education, public expenditure on education and access to higher education by different social or income groups. In particular, the effects on student loan institutions in Latin America of high interest rates, inflation, rising unemployment and the problems of growing burdens of debt should be analysed. Much of the data on which this report is based is inevitably out of date, and more recent information should be collected, at first hand, in developing countries.

Secondly, there is scope for analysis of simple models which show the effects of alternative rates of interest, repayment terms, rates of growth and inflation on the capacity of student loan funds to become self-financing, or to generate a significant flow of finance for higher education. The IDB has developed a model for analysis of student loan programs in its own projects; AID has accumulated considerable information on different student loan programs. Work is in progress in the USA to analyse the effects of alternative assumptions and conditions on student loans. Some of this analysis could yield practical guidelines for student loans in developing countries, and the World Bank is in a position to disseminate the results of such research.

Finally, there is a need to identify countries where experimentation could lead to useful lessons about the applicability of loan programs in developing countries. Experience so far suggest that successful experimentation would require suitable conditions including excess demand for higher education, a substantial difference between social and private rates of return, and between unit costs in higher education and lower levels of the education system, and a political awareness of the importance of financial constraints and a willingness to contemplate unpopular actions. These conditions were found in Ghana in 1971, but unfortunately the scheme seems to have been over-ambitious, and insufficiently planned, in terms of consultation, publicity, and attempts to convince both students and the public of the long run advantages of the change. Certain other countries have considered the introduction of student loans, for example Papua New Guinea and Indonesia.

It will be more difficult to introduce student loans in many

African, Middle Eastern or Asian countries with a tradition of free education, than in Europe or the USA, where student loans represented an extension, rather than a reduction of subsidy. Yet the need is even more urgent. On the subject of political feasibility it is perhaps worth quoting a recent report to the World Bank on Costa Rica:

> "It may be noted here that feasible actions have the effect, following their implementation, of changing the parameters of the system, so that what was previously thought desirable but resisted as unfeasible may come to appear more feasible. In educational systems there are strong conservative forces which develop vested interests in "doing things the way they have always been done", and fear the assumed bad effects of any changes. Once it can be shown that cost-reducing changes can be made without leading to the feared ill effects, then opposition to further cost-saving steps may be lessened.
>
> This in turn leads to the next principle, which is the need for a phased pattern of action to control educational expenditures. Some actions are feasible immediately, other require considerable preparatory work to bring into effect."
> (Wheeler, ACR, 1981, p. 18).

The introduction of student loans in many developing countries falls into the latter category: an action which requires considerable preparatory work. This is particularly true since experience suggests that loans should be accompanied by a policy of fees and other cost reduction exercises. However, the World Bank is in a position to contribute to this preparatory work by a suitable program of research and experimentation.

One way in which experimentation could be encouraged is by the creation of regional organisations, such as the Pan-American Association, APICE, which has helped to stimulate the growth of student loan programs in Latin America. Regional Development Banks could also be encouraged to finance student loans, as the Caribbean Development Bank has done. The first step is to increase awareness of the potential of student loans as a financing mechanism in developing countries.

SECTION X

CONCLUSION : THE FEASIBILITY OF STUDENT LOANS IN DEVELOPING COUNTRIES.

A prediction, made by Rogers in 1971 that "In this decade, many developing countries will move in the direction of achieving greater equity in education through the use of loan programs and other resitrictions on graduates of higher education", has not proved correct. There has been no great increase in the use of student loan programs outside Latin America, and critics have argued that they are inherently infeasible in countries where students and higher education graduates are a priveleged elite, enjoying political power and where features such as inefficient tax collection procedures, and banking mechanisms the importance of the extended family, geographical and job mobility perhaps even a tradition of changing names, would make the collection of loan repayments difficult. These critics also argue that loans will neither generate sufficient revenue to be worthwhile nor change inequalities of access to higher education. The enthusiasm for loan schemes in some developing countries, noted by Rogers and other commentators in the early 1970's, seems to have waned. Yet the increasing financial constraints imposed on government spending on education in both developed and developing countries has recently caused a reawakening of interest.

This report has looked at the actual experience of student loan progams in both developed countries and developing countries, it has looked at the arguments in favour of loans and also at critisms and failures. The conclusion is certainly not a pessimistic one. It must be admitted that the more exaggerated claims of the advocates of student loans have not proved justified, but neither have the exaggerated claims of their detractors. A realistic assessment seems to be that of Augusto Franco Arbelaez, of ICETEX who concluded a review of Latin American experience (in Brodersohn and Sanjurjo, 1978) by declaring his belief that educational credit is a very valuable financing instrument that should be promoted and further developed, but that it should not be considered a panacea for all the ills of higher education, and he suggested that other forms of student aid would still be needed. He suggests that although governments should retain the responsibility for providing the necessary infrastructure for a higher education system, a large part of the current costs of teaching and maintaining universities should be transferred to the beneficiaries, by means of educational credit. He concludes that this will be a long and difficult process, but a battle worth winning for the sake of the future.

It is important to emphasise that student loans are not a panacea, so that policy makers considering the introduction of loans do not have unrealistic expectations. Much of the disillusion over student loans in recent years arose from the fact that too much was expected from the introduction of loans, particularly in terms of equity. Now that there has been a shift of attention in some countries to questions of efficiency and cost recovery, loans may still be rejected on the grounds that they do not offer dramatic improvements in efficiency or quick cost savings.

However, long term savings are worthwile, as well as immediate savings. Although student loans will not solve problems of efficiency and cost recovery they may contribute by increasing cost consciousness among students, and by encouraging them to complete their studies more quickly. Loan repayments will not provide a significant source of funds for higher education in the short run, and indeed may never be completely self-financing. Nevertheless, a system which would allow even half of the present levels of government expenditure on tuition subsidies and scholarships or grants to be recovered, in the long run, from those who derive direct financial benefit from this expenditure is a worthwhile goal for many developing countries.

Another advantage of student loans is that they provide a means of involving the banking system, and private capital, in investment in education, thus reducing the burden on government funds.

Experience with student loan programs supports the argument that "learn now - pay later" is an appropriate philosophy for the individual, and a potentially valuable long-term method of financing higher education for society. It is unlikely that any system could become completely self-financing, and indeed since education clearly brings benefits to society as a whole it is right that it should attract some subsidy. Student loans, combined with fees and interest subsidies, scholarships or loan forgiveness provisions, allow governments to continue to provide subsidies, but on a selective basis, while in the long run a larger share of the costs of education falls on those who derive personal benefit.

The final conclusion of this study, therefore, is that student loans are feasible in developing countries, that they are more equitable than existing patterns of highly subsidised tutition and maintenance for a priveleged minority, and may contribute to greater efficiency by influencing student motivation and cost consciousness. Student loans are flexible, and can be used to provide incentives for particular groups of students or to fulfill manpower objectives. Finally, loans can provide a significant source of finance for higher education, and vocational and technical education in the long run, although but they will not provide quick savings.

The introduction of student loans needs to be carefully planned, accompanied by appropriate changes to fees and, if necessary by cost-reduction measures, and also by an appropriate campaign of publicity to convince both students and taxpayers of the merits of a scheme which allows students financial support today, when they need it, in return for a promise that they, in turn, will contribute directly to the financial support of the students of tomorrow.

Bibliography

Acheampong I.K. "Speech to students at Parliament House, Accra," reported in The Ghanaian Times, June 17, 1972.

Agency for International Development (AID), Dominican Republic: Project Paper (Project No. 517-0127, Loan No. 517-V-036) Washington: AID, 1981.

Aidam, P.K.T. "The University Loan Scheme" The Legon Observer, 12 August 1971, p.9-10.

Arbelaez, A.F. "Objetivos y Administracion del Credito Educativo en America Latina" in Brodersohn, and Sanjurojo, 1978.

Asociacion Panamericana de Instituciones de Credido Educativo (APICE), What is APICE? (APICE Que es?) Bogota, APICE (No date).

Azad, Jagdish Lal, Financing of Higher Education in India, New Delhi: Sterling 1975.

Betancur Mejia, Gabriel, ICETEX: La Experiencia Colombiana De Credito Educativo. Bogota: ICETEX, Mimeo (no date).

Birdsall, N. "Strategies for Analysing Effects of User Charges in the Social Sectors". World Bank. Draft. July 1982.

Bowman, M.J., Millot, B. and Schiefelbein, E. "The Empirical Assessment of Public Support of Higher Education. Studies in Chile, France and Malaysia" World Bank. Education Department. April 1982.

Bowman, M.J. (Editor). Collective Choice in Education. Kluwer-Nijhoff Publishing. 1982.

Brodersohn, Mario and Sanjurjo, Maria Ester, (Editors) Financiamiento de la Educacion en America Latina. Mexico: Fondo de Cultina Economica, IDB, 1978.

Ciller, T. "The Economics of a Service - Loan Program in Financing Higher Education in the Middle East". Higher Education May 1975 (4:2) pp 247-50.

Congressional Budget Office, Federal Student Assistance: Issues and Options, Budget Issue Paper for Fiscal Year 1981, Washington: US Government Printing Office, 1980, p.38.

Council of Ministers of Education, Canada and Secretary of State, Report of the Federal-Provincial Task Force on Student Assistance. Toronto, 1980.

Daniere, Andre, Higher Education in the American Economy. New York: Random House 1964.

Dominguez - Urosa, Jose "Education Financing and Equity: Student Loan Institutions" in Case Study and Exercise Series, Economic Development Institute, World Bank, September 1976.

Dominguez - Urosa, Jose "Prestamos para Estudiar: un analisis du sus usos y limitaciones" in Brohersohn and Sanjurjo, 1978.

Dominguez - Urosa, Jose, Student Loan Institutions in Developing Countries: An Analytical Framework and a Rationale for Their Inclusion in the Banking System, Harvard: Doctor of Education Thesis, 1973.

Dominica Agricultural and Industrial Development Bank, Guidelines for Assistance from Higher Education Loan Fund (Mimeo, no date.)

Dresch, Stephen, "Financial and Behavioural Implications of Federal Student Loan Programs and Proposals" in Tuckman, H.P. and Whaten, E. (Editors) Subsidies to Higher Education: The Issues, New York, Praeger Publishers, 1980.

Dresch, Stephen, "Improving Student Access to the Capital Market: The Fair Access to Higher Education Act" Testimony to Hearings of the U.S. House of Representatives Committee on Education and Labor Sub-committee on Post Secondary Education, June 1979.

Eicher, Jean-Claude, Educational Costing and Financing in Developing Countries : with special reference to Sub-Saharan Africa. World Bank, 1982 (mimeo).

Fields, Gary S. "Private Returns and Social Equity in the Financing of Higher Education" in Court, D and Ghai, D.P. Education, Society and Development: New Perspectives from Kenya. Nairobi: Oxford University Press, 1974 pp.187-197.

Ghana, Republic of, Government Statement on the Students' Loan Scheme, Accra-Tema, Ghana Publishing Corporation, 1971.

Ghana, Republic of, Parliamentary Debates Vol.7, No.17, 7 July 1971.

Ghana, Republic of, Report of Government Committee on the Future Policy for Financial Support for University Students in Ghana. (Under the chairmanship of Mr. Dowuona) Accra-Tema, Ghana Publishing Corporation, 1970.

Gladieux, Lawrence "What Has Congress Wrought?" Change, Vol.12, No.7, October, 1980.

Hartman, Robert, Credit for College: Public Policy for Student Loans. A Report for the Carnegie Commission on Higher Education, New York: McGraw Hill, 1971.

Hauptman, Arthur, M, "Student Loan Defaults: Toward a Better Understanding of the Problem" in Rice, Lois D. (Ed) Student Loans : Problems and Policy Alternatives, New York : College Board, 1977, p.131.

Herrick, Allison, Sharlach, Howard and Seville, Linda, Intercountry Evaluation of Education Credit Institutions in Latin America. Washington: U.S. Agency for International Development, 1974.

Hewagama, L.D., A Study on the University Loan Scheme, Colombo : People's Bank, Sri Lanka, 1978.

Ibacache, Mario Edgardo, El Banco Interamericano de Desarrollo y sus Programas de Credito Educativo, on discusion General de Aspectos Tecnicos Relevantes. Washington : IDB, 1978 (mimeo).

IECE, (Instituto Ecuatoriano de Credito Educativo Y Becas): Efectos Sociales Y Economicos Del Credito Educativo en el Ecuador. Quito: IECE, 1981.

ILO, Growth, Employment and Equity : A Comprehensive Strategy for the Sudan : Report of the ILO/UNDP Employment Mission, Geneva : ILO, 1976.

ILO, First Things First, Meeting the Basic Needs of the People of Nigeria Geneva : ILO, 1981.

Inter-American Development Bank, El Credito Educativo en America Latina April 1976, mimeo.

Inter American Development Bank, News Release
- March 21, 1966 on Loan 88/SF-PN
- December 29, 1970 on Loan 283/SF-JA
- April 22, 1971 on Loan 292/SF-PN
- October 12, 1972 on Loan 336/SF-TT
- March 18, 1976 on Loan 466/SFJA
- December 2, 1976 on Loan 489/SF-HO
- January 19, 1977 on Loan 500/SF-CR
- February 17, 1977 on Loan 503/SF-BA
- September 17, 1981 on Loan 657/SF-HO

Inter-American Development Bank, The Financing of Education in Latin America, Seminar held in Mexico City, November 1978. Washington: IDB.

Israel: The Council for Higher Education, Annual Report, 1980-81 Jerusalem, 1982.

Jallade, Jean-Pierre, The Financing of Education: An Examination of Basic Issues. World Bank Staff Working Paper No. 157, IBRD July 1973.

Jallade, Jean-Pierre, Student Loans in Developing Countries: An Evaluation of the Colombian Performance World Bank Staff Working Paper No. 182 IBRD June 1974.

Jallade, Jean-Pierre, Public Expenditures on Education and Income Distribution in Colombia, Baltimore : John Hopkins Press.

Johnstone D. Bruce, New Patterns for College Lending : Income Contingent Loans, New York : Columbia University Press, 1972.

Kausel, Edgardo Boeninger, "Alternative policies for financing higher education" in IDB, The Financing of Education in Latin America, Washington : IDB, 1978, pp.321-357.

Kulakow, A.M., Brace, J and Morrill, J, *Mobilizing Rural Community Resources for Support and Development of Local Learning Systems in Developing Countries.* Washington: Academy for Educational Development, 1978.

Lee Hansen, W. "Economic Growth and Equal Opportunity : Conflicting or Complementary Goals in Higher Education" August 1982, (mimeo).

Levin, H.M., "Assessing the Equalization Potential of Education". 1982 (mimeo)

Lauglo, Jon, *Universities, National Development and Education.* London : University of London Institute of Education, 1980 (mimeo).

Mbanefoh, G.F. "Sharing the Costs and Benefits of University Education in Nigeria" *Education and Development*, Vol.1, No.2, July 1981, pp.231-243.

McMahon, W.W. and Geske, T.G. (eds) *Financing Education.* University of Illinois Press. 1982.

Morse, J.F., "How We Got Here From There - A Personal Reminiscence of the Early Days." in Rice L.D. (Ed) *Student Loans : Problems and Policy Alternatives.* New York : College Entrance Examination Board, 1977.

Alfonso Ocampo, *Dimensions of Educational Credit* 1982, (mimeo).

Psacharopoulos, G. *Higher Education in Developing Countries: A Cost-Benefit Analysis.* Washington, D.C. World Bank Staff Working Paper No.440, 1980.

Qarz-e-Hasna Scheme for Education : *Operational Rules.* Islamabad 1981 (mimeo).

Renner, R. "The Expansion of Edu-Credit in Latin American Higher Education - Promise or Peril? *Higher Education.* February 1974, pp. 81-90.

Rice, Lois D, (Editor), *Student Loans : Problems and Policy Alternatives,* New York : College Entrance Examination Board, 1977.

Rogers, Daniel, "Financing Higher Education in Less Developed Countries," *Comparative Education Review* Vol.15, February 1971. pp.20-27.

Rogers, Daniel, "Student Loan Programs and the Returns to Investment in Higher Levels of Education in Kenya," *Economic Development and Cultural Change,* January 1972, pp.243-259.

Rogers, Daniel, *A Brief Description of Student Loan Programs in Latin America.* Washington : U.S. Agency for International Development March 1971, mimeo.

Rogers, Daniel, *An Evaluation of Student Loan Programs.* Washington.: U.S. Agency for International Development, February 1972, mimeo.

Rogers, Daniel, *The Economic Effects of Various Methods of Educational Finance* World Bank 1970, (mimeo).

Sanyal, B.C. et.al. University Education and the Labour Market in the Arab Republic of Egypt. Paris : UNESCO/IIEP, 1982.

Tuinder den, B.A.,. Ivory Coast : The Challenge of Success Baltimore : John Hopkins, for the World Bank 1978.

UNESCO (Oficina Regional de Educacion de la UNESCO para America Latina y el Caribe) Informaciones Estadisticas de la Educacion y Analisis Cuantitativo (Informaciones sobre los principales sistemas de credito educativo en 12 paises de America Latina y el Caribe) September 1979, (mimeo).

Wheeler, A.C.R. The Significance of Education in a Structural Adjustment Process in Costa Rica. World Bank, December 1981, (mimeo).

Williams, Peter, "Lending for Learning : An Experiment in Ghana" Minerva, Vol.XII, July 1974, pp. 326-45.

Woodhall, Maureen, Student Loans : A Review of Experience in Scandinavia and Elsewhere. London : George Harrap, 1970.

Woodhall, Maureen, Review of Student Support Schemes in Selected OECD Countries. Paris: O.E.C.D., 1978.

Woodhall, Maureen, Student Loans : Lessons from Recent International Experience. London : Policy Studies Institute, 1982.

World Bank, Education Sector Policy Paper Washington IBRD 1980.

Zymelman, Manuel, Financing and Efficiency in Education : Reference for Administration and Policy making. Harvard University 1973.

APPENDIX 1

SUMMARY OF EDUCATIONAL CREDIT INSTITUTIONS IN LATIN AMERICA

Country and Institutions	Year Established	Sources of Finance (excluding loan repayments)
AGENTINA		
Instituto Nacional de Credito Educativo (INCE)	1969	50% Treasury Ministry of Social Welfare 50% Commercial banks.
BOLIVIA		
Centro Impulsor de Educacion Profesional (CIDEP)		
BRAZIL		
Fonde Nacional de Desarrollo de la Educacion (FNDE)	1968	Tax incentives Federal Lottery Bank Deposits
Caixa Economica Federal	1976	Federal Sport Lottery Bank of Brazil Petrobras (state owned oil company).
Associagas dos Profissionais Liberais Universitarios de Brasil (APLUB) (non-profit making private trade union institution)	1971	Fees to institutions for services Donations from APLUB
COLOMBIA		
Instituto Colombiano de Credito Educativo y Estudios Technicos en el Exterior (ICETEX)	1950	Government funds Administration of Enterprise Funds Bank Loans Central Bank IDB

COSTA RICA

Comision Nacional de Prestamos para Educacion (CONAPE)	1965	Central Bank Government funds IDB

CHILE

Junta Nacional de Auxilio Escolar y Becas (JNAEB)	1964	Social Security contributions Government funds.
Catholic University of Chile		

ECUADOR

Instituto Ecuatoriano de Credito Educativo y Becas (IECE)	1971	Government funds oil revenues Payroll Tax

EL SALVADOR

Fondo de Garantia para el Credito Educativo (EDUCREDITO)		Government Funds
Fonde de Desarrollo Economico (FDE)		Central Bank

HONDURAS

EDUCREDITO	1968	Government Funds IDB AID

JAMAICA

Students Loan Bureau	1971	Government Funds Bank of Jamaica IDB

MEXICO

Consejo Nacional de Formento Educativo (CONAFE)	1971	

Banco de Mexico Eficine de Credito Educativo	1965	Federal Government Bank of Mexico
NICARAGUA		
Instituto Nicaraguense de Desarrolla (INDE)	1963	Private donations AID
PANAMA		
Instituto para la Formacion y Aprovechamiento de los Recursos Humanos IFARHU	1965	Government Funds Payroll Tax (Education Insurance) IDB
PERU		
Instituto Peruano de Fomento Educativo (IPFE)	1962	Donations Bank Loans AID
Instituto Nacional de Becas y Credito Educativo (INABEC)	1973	Government Funds
DOMINICAN REPUBLIC		
Fundacion de Credito Educativo (FCE)	1964	Government Funds AID Donations
VENEZUELA		
EDUCREDITO	1965	Government Funds Donations
Sociedad Administradora de Credito Educativo para la Universidad de Oriente (SACEUDO)	1969	Government and Regional Funds

World Bank Publications of Related Interest

Alternative Routes to Formal Education: Distance Teaching for School Equivalency
edited by Hilary Perraton

The demand for education is outstripping the capacity of many countries to build schools or to recruit and pay teachers. To meet this demand and to provide access to education to individuals who are unable to attend regular schools, educators throughout the world are trying to develop alternatives to the traditional classroom. One of these alternatives—known as distance teaching—combines correspondence courses with radio or television broadcasts and occasional face-to-face study.

Does this alternative work? Is it cheaper? This book is the first attempt to answer such key questions. It examines the variety of ways in which distance teaching has been used, provides comparisons of specific cases, analyzes their costs, and considers the effectiveness of distance teaching versus traditional education.

The Johns Hopkins University Press. 1982. 344 pages.

LC 82-7233. ISBN 0-8018-2587-3, $35.00 (£26.25) hardcover.

Worker-Peasant Education in the People's Republic of China
Nat J. Colletta

Reviews and analyzes adult education activities in China from the late 1920s to the current time.

World Bank Staff Working Paper No. 527. 1982. 94 pages.

ISBN 0-8213-0050-4. $3.00.

Publishing for Schools: Textbooks and the Less Developed Countries
Peter H. Neumann

World Bank Staff Working Paper No. 398. June 1980. ii + 79 pages (including 2 appendixes).

Stock No. WP-0398. $3.00.

Attacking Rural Poverty: How Non-Formal Education Can Help
Philip H. Coombs and Manzoor Ahmed

Educational efforts outside the formal school system that offer potential for rural development and productivity.

The Johns Hopkins University Press, 1974; 3rd paperback printing, 1980. 310 pages (including 3 appendixes, references, index).

LC 73-19350. ISBN 0-8018-1600-9, $25.00 (£11.00) hardcover; ISBN 0-8018-1601-7, $10.95 (£4.25) paperback.

Spanish: La lucha contra la pobreza rural: el aporte de la educación no formal. *Editorial Tecnos, 1975.*

ISBN 84-309-0559-6, 725 pesetas.

Cost-Benefit Analysis in Education: A Case Study of Kenya
Hans Heinrich Thias and Martin Carnoy

Attempts to measure the benefits of various types of education in monetary terms, and to assess the role of earnings in the demand for and supply of educated people in a country.

The Johns Hopkins University Press, 1972. 208 pages (including 5 annexes, bibliography).

LC 72-187064. ISBN 0-8018-1335-2, $6.95 (£4.25) paperback.

The Economic Evaluation of Vocational Training Programs
Manuel Zymelman

A methodology for appraising the cost effectiveness of alternative methods of industrial training in developing countries.

The Johns Hopkins University Press, 1976. 134 pages (including chart, 3 appendixes, bibliography).

LC 76-4868. ISBN 0-8018-1855-9, $6.00 (£3.50) paperback.

Spanish: Programas de formación profesional: su evaluación económica. *Editorial Tecnos, 1977.*

ISBN 84-309-0747-5, 415 pesetas.

Education
Wadi D. Haddad, coordinating author

Emphasizes the pervasive role of education in development and draws extensively on the Bank's experience in education for two decades and its close collaborative ties with other international agencies, individuals, and institutions of developing countries.

Sector Policy Paper. April 1980. 143 pages (including 19 annexes, map). English, French, Spanish, Japanese, and Arabic.

Stock Nos. PP-8002-E, PP-8002-F, PP-8002-S, PP-8002-J, PP-8002-A. $5.00.

The Educational Use of Mass Media
Gloria Feliciano, Alan Hancock, Gerald Hein, Albert Horley, Janet Jenkins, Wallace Lambert, Hilary Perraton, Takashi Sakamoto, Nelly Sidoti, John Tiffin, and Shigenari Futagami

Deals with the issues that developing country educators and decisionmakers encounter when they consider using mass media to further the country's education and development.

World Bank Staff Working Paper No. 491. October 1981. v + 124 pages (including bibliography).

Stock No. WP-0491. $5.00.

The Use of First and Second Languages in Primary Education: Selected Case Studies
Nadine Dutcher

Addresses some areas of concern regarding the appropriate language for initial primary education in multilingual societies. Reviews eight case studies in seven countries in which primary schooling was given either in the second language or in the first and compares achievement in reading and arithmetic. Concludes that the best choice of language must be determined on a case-by-case basis depending on the interrelated characteristics of each situation.

World Bank Staff Working Paper No. 504. January 1982. iii + 62 pages (including annex, references).

Stock No. WP-0504. $3.00.

Education and Basic Human Needs
Abdun Noor

Conceptualizes basic education and examines its ability to help the poor acquire skills that enable them to meet their basic needs. Groups countries into four major categories and suggests policy choices—based on the unique socioeconomic circumstances in each category—that will make basic education universal by the year 2000.

World Bank Staff Working Paper No. 450. April 1981. iv + 64 pages (including 2 annexes).

Stock No. WP-0450. $3.00.

Education and Income
Edited by Timothy King; prepared by Mary Jean Bowman, George Psacharopoulos, Marlaine E. Lockheed, Dean T. Jamison, Lawrence J. Lau, Albert Berry, and Gary S. Fields.

World Bank Staff Working Paper No. 402. July 1980. viii + 315 pages (including appendix, bibliography).

Stock No. WP-0402. $15.00.

Education Programs and Projects: Analytical Techniques, Case Studies, and Exercies
Irving A. Sirken

World Bank (EDI), January 1977; revised edition, 1979. ix + 287 pages. (Available from ILS, 1715 Connecticut Avenue, N.W., Washington, D.C. 20009, U.S.A.) $6.00 paperback.

The Effects of Education on Health
Susan H. Cochrane and others

World Bank Staff Working Paper No. 405. July 1980. 95 pages.

Stock No. WP-0405. $3.00.

The Evaluation of Human Capital in Malawi
Stephen P. Heyneman

World Bank Staff Working Paper No. 420. October 1980. vi + 101 pages (including references, 21 tables, 6 annexes).

Stock No. WP-0420. $5.00.

Farmer Education and Farm Efficiency
Dean T. Jamison and Lawrence J. Lau

This book complements earlier studies by reviewing existing literature on the relation between farmer education and farm efficiency. The authors then are able to confirm these earlier findings—which strongly suggest that the more educated farmers are more productive, particularly where new inputs and methods are available—by using new techniques to examine new data sets from Korea, Malaysia, and Thailand. Price data from Thailand are used to test the effect of education on the ability of a farmer to adjust the prices and composition of his output to the prevailing prices.

The Johns Hopkins University Press, 1982. 310 pages (including bibliography, appendixes, index).

LC 81-47612. ISBN 0-8018-2575-X, $27.50 hardcover.

Higher Education in Developing Countries: A Cost-Benefit Analysis
George Psacharopoulos

World Bank Staff Working Paper No. 440. November 1980. 129 pages (including references, tables).

Stock No. WP-0440. $5.00.

NEW

Mexico's Free Textbooks —Nationalism and the Urgency to Educate
Peter H. Neumann and Maureen A. Cunningham

World Bank Staff Working Paper No. 541. 1982. 148 pages.

ISBN 0-8213-0101-2. $5.00.

Primary Schooling and Economic Development: A Review of the Evidence
Christopher Colclough

World Bank Staff Working Paper No. 399. June 1980. 31 pages (including references, 5 tables).

Stock No. WP-0399. $3.00.

Primary School Participation and Its Internal Distribution in Eastern Africa
Jack van L. Maas and Bert Criel

Examines the distribution of primary school enrollments within and among the countries of the Eastern Africa Region.

World Bank Staff Working Paper No. 511. August 1982. 105 pages.

ISBN 0-8213-0055-5. $5.00.

Public Expenditures on Education and Income Distribution in Colombia
Jean-Pierre Jallade

Examines the allocation of educational benefits among various population groups and considers the distributional effects of taxes that pay for public subsidies in general.

The Johns Hopkins University Press, 1974. 90 pages (including 2 annexes, bibliography).

LC 74-4216. ISBN 0-8018-1628-9, $5.00 (£3.00) paperback.

REPRINTS

The Economics of Higher Education in Developing Countries
George Psacharopoulos

World Bank Reprint Series: Number 225. Reprinted from Comparative Education Review, vol. 26, no. 2 (June 1982):139-59.

Stock No. RP-0225. Free of charge.

The Optimal Ability-Education Mix and the Misallocation of Resources within Education: Magnitude for Developing Countries
Sebastian Pinera and Marcelo Selowsky

World Bank Reprint Series: Number 192. Reprinted from Journal of Development Economics, vol. 8 (1981):111-31.

Stock No. RP-0192. Free of charge.

Returns to Education: An Updated International Comparison
George Psacharopoulos

World Bank Reprint Series: Number 210. Reprinted from Comparative Education, vol. 17, no. 3, 1981.

Stock No. RP-0210. Free of charge.

The Returns to Education: Increasing with Experience or Decreasing with Expansion?
J.B. Knight and R.H. Sabot

World Bank Reprint Series: Number 200. Reprinted from Oxford Bulletin of Economics and Statistics, vol. 43, no. 1 (February 1981):51-71.

Stock No. RP-0200. Free of charge.

WORLD BANK PUBLICATIONS
ORDER FORM

SEND TO:
WORLD BANK PUBLICATIONS
P.O. BOX 37525
WASHINGTON, D.C. 20013
U.S.A.

or

WORLD BANK PUBLICATIONS
66, AVENUE D'IÉNA
75116 PARIS, FRANCE

Name: _____

Address: _____

_____

Stock or ISBN #	Author, Title	Qty.	Price	Total

Sub-Total Cost: _____

Postage & handling fee for more than two free items ($1.00 each): _____

Total copies: _____ Air mail surcharge ($2.00 each): _____

TOTAL PAYMENT ENCLOSED: _____

Make checks payable: WORLD BANK PUBLICATIONS

Prepayment on orders from individuals is requested. Purchase orders are accepted from booksellers, library suppliers, libraries, and institutions. All prices include cost of postage by the least expensive means. The prices and publication dates quoted in this Catalog are subject to change without notice.

No refunds will be given for items that cannot be filled. Credit will be applied towards future orders.

No more than two free publications will be provided without charge. Requests for additional copies will be filled at a charge of US $1.00 per copy to cover handling and postage costs.

Airmail delivery will require a prepayment of US $2.00 per copy.

Mail-order payment to the World Bank need not be in U.S. dollars, but the amount remitted must be at the rate of exchange on the day the order is placed. The World Bank will also accept Unesco coupons.